Challe
2016

The Women's Initiative
1101 East High Street, Suite A
Charlottesville, VA 22902
www.thewomensinitiative.org
434.872.0047

Copyright 2017 The Women's Initiative

1st Edition

ISBN 978-1-365-68684-9

All rights reserved. This book may not be reproduced, in whole or in part, in any form or by any means electronic or mechanical, including photocopying, recording or by any information storage and retrieval system now known or hereafter invented, without written permission from The Women's Initiative.

Challenge into Change

2016 Writing Contest

Printed in USA by Lulu Press.

You may order this title through Lulu.com, Amazon.com, Barnesandnoble.com or by calling

The Women's Initiative 434.872.0047.

DEDICATION
ℰℴℭℛ

This book is dedicated to Amy Lane,
Business and Marketing Manager of The Women's Initiative,
without whose tireless, year-round work this project
would not be possible, and whose veneration—and
embodiment—of the spirit of Challenge into Change
is an example to us all.

ABOUT THE WOMEN'S INITIATIVE

The Women's Initiative is a nonprofit in Charlottesville, Virginia, that provides vital mental health services to women regardless of their ability to pay. Our counseling services, social support and education enable women to transform life challenges into positive change and growth. We serve area women who struggle with a range of mental health needs and who lack access to effective care due to factors such as race, ethnicity, economic disadvantage, sexual orientation or gender identity, illness, language, age and disability. We believe every woman has an innate capacity for healing that, once uncovered and directed, results in better mental and physical health.

Visit us at www.thewomensinitiative.org

empowering women in times of challenge & change

TABLE OF CONTENTS

Introduction 1

About Challenge into Change 3

Pretty Brown Girl (1ˢᵗ Place) *Aerial Perkins* 5

Chronic Guest (2ⁿᵈ Place) *Kaity L. Yang* 8

Alive (3ʳᵈ Place) *Becca Pizmoht* 11

Mi Segunda Oportunidad (My Second Chance)

      Carmen Alcantra 14

Deprived Woman from Education *Aleena* 18

That Which Is Lost, Then Reclaimed *Mary Anderson* 20

Finding Strength in Pain *Anna* 23

Second Chance *Anonymous* 24

Survivor *Anonymous* 26

Womanessence *Anonymous* 28

Los Angeles Ayudan (When Angels Help) *Otilia Arroyo* 29

Failure *Beverly B.* 33

Tribute to My Mother *Rosemary Balister* 35

Untitled *Rachael Ballard* 37

Where I'm From *Rebecca Ballard* 38

My Life Story *Irene Barbera* 40

I Am the Face *Allison Barnes* 41

Some Women *Frances Curtis Barnhart* 43

Dios Te Bendiga y Te Llene de Victoria (God Blesses You and Fills You with Victories) *Liliana Bedoya*........................ 46

Day by Day by *Elle M. Bergert* 50

Blossom in Wood *Joncey Boggs*.. 53

Divorce Laugh to Keep from Crying *Sheila Boling* 55

Spirit of Being Me *Katherine A. Borges* 58

Pilgrimage *Brittany*... 61

A New Me *Brenda Brown-Grooms*....................................... 63

Loving You! The Day of Sunshine! *Patricia Burley-Choloski* 65

A Family Legacy *Debbie Calabretta*.................................. 67

Grand Mothers *Monique Collins Carey*................................ 69

My Promise *Janet Centini* 71

No Hay Tiempo Para Llorar (There's No Time for Tears)
Lilian Cerna 73

The Journey of Life *Eleanor L. Crichlow* 79

Got Lemons? Make Lemonade! *Jill Watson Clark*...................... 81

She Is Me *Carnegie Clatterbaugh* 84

The Lost Child *Brianna Cousins*..................................... 86

Taking the Scenic Route *Stephanie Rose DeNicola* 89

Against All Odds *Marian Dixon*...................................... 91

The Angel *Mary Dudley Eggleston* 93

My Tutor and My Friend *Sharon W. Eldridge* 95

For Steve, but Really for Me *Elizabeth*............................. 97

My Mother's News *Dabney Farmer*..99

From Couch Surfing to Skydiving - A Tale of Surviving

Domestic Violence *B. Faulkner*..102

The Meaning of Her Rain *Veronica Haunani Fitzhugh*...............105

Desperation *Ebony Fletcher*...107

My Past Life *Kamila FNU*...109

Learning to Like the Unlikeable *June Forte* 112

Una Familia que Emigra a USA (A Family that Migrates to the

US) *Maria Godoy*..114

I WASN'T GOOD ENOUGH *Tanya Denise Gordon*.................120

Bits N Pieces *Sekina L. Greene* 122

SHE IS MY MOM! *Waheda Haidari*....................................124

Pray Your Way Up *Peggy Jean Hatton*................................126

Boots, Boobs and Mojo *Shaaron Honeycutt* 128

INSANITY *j*...130

Discovering My Calling, Securing My Future

Valerie R. Jackson..133

Long Way Home *Eilise Johnson*...136

Birth Trauma is Real *Brianne Kirkpatrick*...........................138

Dear Aunt Mary, *Nina Knight*...141

May *Audrey Kocher*..143

Changing through Dream Work *Phyllis R. Koch-Sheras, PhD*...146

Never. Give. Up. *Krista* 148

Presence *Meredith Largiader*...150

You Are *Donna Lloyd* 152

Undefined *Priya Mahadevan* 154

Greedy for an Education *Michelle McSherrey* 157

Twice Delivered *Jeanette Meade* 160

FULL CIRCLE *Allyson Mescher* 162

Anxiety *Patricia W. Pollock* 164

Standing for the Silent *Jojo Robertson* 166

I Am, That I Am *Mary Rodwell* 169

Remembering Irene *Michele J. Rolle* 171

Explosive Material Is Best Treated with Prayer! *Amelia Rose* .. 174

Dutch Tulips *Dylan Roth* 176

Youthful Grievances *Kieran Rundle* 178

Finding What's Eating Me *Sera S.* 182

Follow Your Dreams? *Sharon Showalter* 185

Ms. Maitreya, a Haiku *Slavin* 187

Escribiendo mi Historia, el Diario de una Mexicana

(Writing My Story, the Diary of a Mexican Woman)

    Coco Sotelo 188

Untitled *Stormi* 194

Kleenex for Lace *Maura Tierney* 196

Court Square Chestnut *Sue Tiezzi* 198

Dysphoria *Roxana Trujillo* 200

Bunny *Erin Tucker* 204

I Am . . . *Shrika Turner* 206

Within ME *Nancy Utz* 208

Untitled *Scott Van Dorn* 209

Seniors on the Move *Louella J. Walker* 211

Solid Oak *Erin Newton Wells* 213

Acknowledgements 217

Meet Our Judges 219

INTRODUCTION
ℬℭ

*"You start out with one thing, end
up with another, and nothing's
like it used to be, not even the future."*
—Rita Dove, from "O"

At The Women's Initiative, we believe in the inherent wisdom and healing capacity of storytelling. Over millennia, women have gathered and used words, written and sung, to share information, pass down lore, uplift, and remember. As the agency celebrates its ten-year anniversary, it is natural to reflect on the ways in which our nation, communities, and people have changed and what our role is in shaping a future we want to live in.

The past year in particular has been the embodiment of what Challenge into Change has come to mean to us: The capacity to look at a mountain and see not defeat but a bridge to be crossed using radical love of one another and fierce compassion. The Women's Initiative aims to be a part of that bridge, and offers the Challenge into Change Writing Contest as a platform for women's voices and women's stories. We hope it can be a beacon of truth amidst confusion, a testimony to the beauty of our shared experiences, and most importantly a tool for healing.

This year's contest drew more than double the number of participants of any other in the history of the agency. We believe this reflects the growing need for sharing, reshaping, and learning from our own narratives. If our current socio-political climate tells us anything, it is that although we live and work together, we do not truly know the stories of our neighbors, colleagues, and sometimes friends and family. Having read the stories submitted to this year's volume, I feel assured that one response to this, and a recipe for the future we can't see yet, lies within these pages filled with vulnerability, strength, and resilience.

Eboni Bugg, LCSW
Program Director

ABOUT CHALLENGE INTO CHANGE
✂ ℘℧ ✂

Challenge into Change is a forum for real-life stories about women overcoming personal struggles. In the fall of 2016, The Women's Initiative invited Central Virginians to submit a poem or essay of 500 words or less about a woman (themselves or someone they knew) who had surmounted a difficult situation in her life. Eighty-six writers responded to our call. This is their book.

Challenge into Change began in 2008 as a celebration of The Women's Initiative's first year of providing vital mental health services to women regardless of ability to pay. Since then, it has become a venue for veteran and emerging writers alike to showcase their talents and engage in creative exploration. As The Women's Initiative marks its tenth year in Charlottesville, we present this volume—a chorus of voices from the community—as a testament to what lies at the heart of our agency's vision: women's capacity for healing.

How to read this book

This volume opens with the works of our three winners, who each receive cash prizes and read their work at the 2017 Festival of the Book. How do we determine who wins? An independent panel of judges evaluates each submission blind. The panel rewards writing that has emotional resonance and clearly communicates how its subject manifested challenge out of a challenging life situation. The panel also looks for stories that effectively use language to convey meaning, and have the power to motivate and encourage others.

Happily, this is a difficult task for our judges, as these qualities can be found throughout this book. As you read, make sure to take in the comments provided by our judges and additional readers, which follow each entry. These responses reflect on the unique gift each piece offers us and continue the conversation that each writer has started. It is our hope that, for the writers and for you, these conversations are the start of something sustaining and healing.

Challenge into Change

Challenge into Change

Pretty Brown Girl
Aerial Perkins

First Place

I pressed my face to the window. My vision blurred by the waterfall of tears I cannot seem to control. The school bus comes to a screeching halt and kids get off but I refuse to let them see my face. "Oreo cookie, Oreo cookie, Oreo cookie!" was still ringing in my ears. At this very moment the embarrassment of being dark skin was pouring right through my small ten year old body. I wish I could hide but the only solace was the over-sized red hoodie I was wearing. I buried myself in it until the chanting ceased.

Four years later

My hands are crying with blood and fatigue. The mirror unscathed by my rage and anger stares back at me. Phrases like: "you're pretty...for a dark skin girl", "if only you were two shades lighter", "the blacker the berry the sweeter the juice" made me scream "I hate you" to the mirror. "I hate you, I hate you...I hate you!" I melted to the bathroom floor breathless and sobbing. I am barely through my freshman year of high school and the only person who has ever told me I was beautiful died months ago. My grandfather meant it too and at the time, I didn't believe him.

Ten years later

I picked up People Magazine as I stand at the counter to pay for my groceries. Lupita Nyong'o graces the cover as "People's Most Beautiful Person". I squealed with excitement but was quickly reminded of where I was as I felt the stares of the people around me. I paid for my stuff including the magazine and rushed home.

"Mom look!" Barely able to contain my excitement I pushed the magazine at her. "She is dark skin like me!!" My mom acknowledges me

Challenge into Change

with a smile too busy on her Kindle to match my enthusiasm. I ran to the bathroom mirror, the same mirror that reduced me to tears ten years ago, and ran my fingers through the hair I had left. Just like Nyong'o, I cut my hair short and natural and I have never felt more beautiful.

Now

The natural light coming through the stunning wooden windows gave the studio good vibes. I place my colorful yoga mat on the floor and watch beautiful women of color fill the space. The sense of belonging overwhelmed me as we flowed through the vinyasa sequence. As I take warrior two pose I begin to reflect over the years where I felt angry, sad and weak because of what I believe to be a deformity. My brown skin was the target of relentless bullying. Now my brown skin is complimented more often. I see women like Lupita Nyong'o, Michelle Obama, my yoga teacher, and my mom and realize that the essence of my beauty is not just my smile, my brown eyes, or my hair…it is the self-confidence on the inside that generates beauty. I am a pretty brown girl.

How our judges and readers responded…

Brave and clear. ♥ *Passionate, immediate writing makes the past come alive.* ♥ *Arresting vignettes.* ♥ *In the beginning, the writer speaks of her skin as dark. However, when she speaks of where she is now as it relates to her complexion, she says her skin in "brown". To me, this clearly shows the change of mindset. Brown is more of a positive to her than dark. As her self-confidence grew, how she referred to herself and her skin changed.* ♥ *The succinct brilliance of this piece drives its reader from a place of despair and frustration to confidence and power.* ♥ *It inspires all of us to be proud of who we are, including the body with which we have been graced.*

BIO:

Aerial Perkins is a twenty-four-year-old aspiring writer and photographer. She was born in Charlottesville but was raised in Buckingham County, Virginia. Aerial has two poems, one Challenge into Change story and a photograph published. She is a blogger who writes and advocates for Adoptee rights. She hopes in the future to publish a memoir and more photography. When she is not working, writing or taking photos you can find her smiling or randomly dancing to her favorite music.

Chronic Guest
Kaity L. Yang

Second Place

Self-compassion is foreign
To me.
Self-love is a stranger
In my house, in my
Body. Nobody mentioned
Abuse

Dressed as negative self-talk,
She occupied my mind. My chronic guest
Dirtied my windows, clouded
What little light I possessed

Twice I failed
To extinguish
My light – first overdose, Valium – second overdose, Klonopin

Brought on by internalizing
Messages from my mother

YOU
Are a disappointment –
LEFTOVER!
Shame you bring, you unmarried!

YOU
Are a bad daughter –
Too much school, fancy paper, no man!
Shame you bring, you unmarried!

YOU
Do not love your mother –

Selfish brat, no grandchildren!
Shame you bring, you unmarried!

YOU
Are man's plaything –
To have and to hold! Did you forget your role as woman?
My chronic guest reminded me

Vision blurry, voice unsure
I evicted my chronic guest. Wiped my eyes clean and repeated –

I
Am good enough. And
I matter. I
Am worthy.

As I vacuumed away self-hatred
And cast open rusty windows, encrusted with salt. Fresh air
Poured in like concrete.
Welcome back, little light

I
Am loved. And
I have value. I
Am worthy.

I
Am my own.
To have and to hold. I
Am worthy.

I
Am proud of this house.
This body. This face. This mind. I
Am worthy.

Challenge into Change

This is my letter of love. A peek
Into my house. That darkness, that chronic guest.
Dearly departed, replaced with
Light.

May she be a beacon for you, too.

How our judges and readers responded...

You describe the departure of depression so movingly. It is wonderful that Light has replaced Darkness for you. ♥ *Powerful, courageous, compelling. Brave and honest—and anguished—engages the reader throughout.* ♥ *Excellently written piece. You can feel her go from a woman of low self-esteem to a woman who finds her inner strength and self-confidence.* ♥ *In this poem, the author uses cadence and repetition to portray a transformation from weakness to strength.* ♥ *Each of us must look inside to the doubts within and find a mantra that gives us sustenance and inspiration. Here, in this piece, the author lets us see how such a mantra is created and gives us our own way forward.*

BIO:

Kaity L. Yang is a 28-year-old Gates Millennium Scholar and double University of Virginia alumnus who practices resilience every day. A survivor of multiple traumas and abuse which led to mental illness, Yang persevered to the bewilderment of many. She lost her father unexpectedly to cancer at age 6, cares for her emotionally toxic, illiterate, refugee mother, cheated death in a car wreck at age 22, and survived rape. Yang wishes to serve as a beacon of hope.

Alive

Becca Pizmoht

Third Place

I almost skipped my annual mammogram. I had several years of uneventful images and June was extremely busy. Had I found the phone number, I would have canceled or postponed my annual exam. But I didn't. On June 24th, exactly 365 days from my last mammogram, I went for the annual screening. Three days later, driving home from a court hearing in Richmond that I was covering for the local paper, I received a call from the hospital telling me to come back for a recheck...something was slightly abnormal.

It wasn't until the surgeon called with the results of my biopsy that the reality hit. He called it invasive ductile carcinoma. I wasn't ready to be a cancer patient, was I? After all I ate well, kept fit and healthy; my primary means of making a living was riding and training horses, I ran 5K and 10K races almost every weekend, I didn't feel bad, how could I have cancer?

But I did.

And then in August, I had a lumpectomy and the cancer and affected lymph nodes were removed. And my life went on. Only my family and closest friends knew what was happening. I was determined not to let my illness define my life. It didn't. I was back at work and riding as soon as my stitches were removed. Two weeks after surgery, I ran in a 5K.

About a month after surgery I started chemotherapy. I was still determined that cancer and treatment were not going to define my life. I was going to live and work like everything was normal. And pretty much it was. There were days that I felt like I had drunk a liter of tequila the night before but I got up and pretended that everything was fine. No matter how nauseous or tired I tried to smile and just go on.

My hair fell out. I thought I'd be ready for it but it was a shock for it to come out in clumps. My co-workers shaved my head and I covered it up with a scarf. The lack of hair made for a few awkward moments. Twice people stopped to tell me how nice it was that I had shaved my head in support of someone going through cancer treatment. The first time I smiled, the second time I told them that I had breast cancer.

I kept running. Slowly. Gone are my 7:30 miles, for now I'm content with 9 minute miles and it's ok. Just hearing my feet hit the pavement reassures me that I'm alive.

I pushed to start radiation, the next phase of treatment so that I can have as much billed to my insurance this year. The drive is maddening and takes a big block of the day. I still strive to have a normal day, to get up and feed the animals and go to work. The shadow that is cancer is there but it won't darken my day.

I am alive.

How our judges and readers responded…

People talk of battles with cancer, and you describe so exactly your own struggle. Your writing can be a source of courage for others. ♥ *This is powerful in its restraint, in fact it is powerful because of its restraint which bespeaks courage and strength.* ♥ *There is absolutely no sense of "why me," or victimhood. Very persuasive. Emotional impact from a straightforward account.* ♥ *I admire this writer's restraint. How do you press forward in times of great strife and pain?* ♥ *In this piece, the author presents clearly the choices before us when we encounter illness and tragedy in our lives. In tightly-composed prose, the protagonist's journey inspires us to give everything we have even when the circumstances appear most challenging.*

BIO:

Becca Pizmoht lives in Rapidan, VA with her husband Roman and 2 dogs, 1 cat and 1 horse. She works as a horse trainer and writer for the Madison Eagle and is currently undergoing cancer treatment at Martha Jefferson Hospital and trying to pursue as normal a life as possible.

Mi Segunda Oportunidad
Carmen Alcantara

Pienso que la vida te da muchas oportunidades, está en nosotros alcanzarlas.

Me llamo Carmen y soy bien peruana como la mazamorra morada. Toda esta aventura comienza, cuando viajé a Alemania por un intercambio cultural, luego regresé a mi país, terminé mi profesión, me licencié como maestra de primaria, me casé y tuve dos hijos bellos.

Mi madre, sin querer talvez, hizo diferencias entre hermanos y a mí me tocó la peor parte. No tenía un espacio donde construir una vivienda para mi familia. Mi esposo no tenía trabajo seguro y es allí donde se le presenta una oportunidad de trabajo en Virginia, USA. Yo lo animé, entusiasmé, motivé y apoyé. Hace meses que el llego acá. La distancia nos maltrató emocionalmente y por consecuente también a mis hijos.

Decidí estar junto a él. Dejé mi trabajo, mis colegas, familiares, amigos y mi país. Lo alcancé hace poco.

Ahora vivimos en Culpeper en unión, paz y armonía. Mis hijos estudiando, mi esposo trabajando y yo estudiando inglés, pronto serviré como voluntaria y encontrare un trabajo para apoyar a mi hogar.

Cómo respondieron nuestros jueces y lectores...

En tu historia has logrado describir maravillosamente los sacrificios y la valentía de un inmigrante al dejar todo en su país y venir a los Estados Unidos en busca de una 'segunda oportunidad'. Asimismo, resaltas las decisiones tan difíciles que muchos inmigrantes tienen que tomar para mantener sus familias unida. ♥ *¡Mucha suerte en todos tus planes futuros!* ♥ *Bienvenidos a América y a Virginia. Estas determinada a hacer realidad tus sueños aquí, y tienes la capacidad de conseguir lo que desees.*

Biografía:

Mi nombre es Carmen Irene Alcantara natural de Lima capital de Peru. Tengo 45 años gloriosos, naci el 17 de julio de 1971. Soy profesora licenciada en educacion primaria. Felizmente casada con Oscar Zapata y tengo dos hijos varones de 9 y 7 años. Me encanta hacer ejercicios leer y escribir.

My Second Chance

(English translation from Spanish)
Carmen Alcantara

I truly believe life offers us plenty of opportunities and that it is up to us to be able to reach them.

My name is Carmen and I am as Peruvian as the "mazamorra morada" (purple corn pudding). This great adventure starts when I traveled to Germany as part of a cultural exchange program. Upon my return to Peru I graduated as an Elementary School teacher, got married and had two beautiful children.

My mother, maybe without realizing it, treated my siblings and me very differently and I feel I got the worst out of it. I did not have a space in which to build a home for my family and my husband did not have insurance. Soon after that, a great opportunity presented itself in the form of a work opportunity in Virginia, USA. I encouraged him, motivated him and supported him through this decision. He came to the US a couple of months ago. I feel that the distance emotionally hurt me and my children; therefore, I decided to be with him, I left my job, my colleagues, my friends, my family and my country and I came to the US to be with him.

We now reside in Culpeper and we live in union, peace and harmony. My children are attending school, my husband is currently working and I am learning English. I look forward to becoming a volunteer and I am planning to find a job in order to support our home.

How our judges and readers responded…

In your story, you have beautifully described the sacrifices and courage of an immigrant leaving everything in your country and coming to the United States in search of a 'second chance' in life. You also highlight the difficult decisions many immigrants have to make in order to keep their families together. ♥ *Good luck in all your future plans!* ♥ *Welcome to America and to Virginia. You are determined to realize your dreams here, and you have the capacity to achieve what you wish for.*

BIO:

My name is Carmen Irene Alcantara. I am from Lima, the capital of Peru. I am 45 glorious years old, born on July 17, 1971. I am a licensed teacher in primary education. Happily married to Oscar Zapata and I have two sons, ages 9 and 7. I love doing exercises, reading and writing.

Deprived Woman from Education
Aleena

A black cloud of pain is hovering over her with strong winds that want to take her with it, but she is holding so firmly to it that doesn't want to lose it. It's her life, her future, her passion. She wants to be successful and knowledgeable like a boy, like her male cousins that have every opportunity provided for them. "Why can't I have, why can't I be treated like them? " she said. She knew her answer because she was taught to be weaker than boys and she's worthless due to her gender, but despite all of them, she still had the desire to be considered as a human being and someone that has the same right as a boy. When she was 12, she was deprived of going to school because women don't need education. Women have no rights to have knowledge, otherwise, they would be disobedient to their brother, father, or male that are superior to them. On the other hand, her male cousins that didn't want to study, skip school, and get Fs in all their subject were praised and had facilitated everything for them. "Why can I not go to school, why should I stay home, cook, clean, and take care of the house?", she said. I had no response to that question and I couldn't comfort her because I was afraid of that situation and that I might one day can't go to school, too. The tears that were dropping down her cheeks weren't only hers, I could feel them, and I could understand because I was seeing myself in that situation in two or three years. When I saw her crying and couldn't go to school anymore, I was praying not to get older because I didn't want to get in that situation. A year passed, and she is home, cooking, cleaning, and taking care of home, while her male cousins brought their report cards that had failed all their classes and had to be in that grade again. Nobody told anything to them, they were praising them with tenderness, kindness, whereas her, they were ordering her to go cook for them and clean up the house. I closely observed her gentle behaviour and her humble voice accepting that she couldn't do anything than listening to their commands. The day passed with the burden of inequality and unfairness. Nobody was there to realise, maybe some were, but they had no authority and ability to do anything either. The night came, and she put her head down on her pillow with the blanket over her, with the hope to be able to continue her education and go to school. In the morning, she was sweeping in front of their house and saw me going to school. She looked at me with admiration and gave a valuable advice, which was always try to fight against injustice and inequality. You should try to be someone that would prove them wrong and here I'm a junior high.

How our judges and readers responded...

You have a really intense, forceful voice, and you clearly articulate the sense of injustice that you have felt throughout your life. ♥ *The story takes a wonderful turn toward affirmation of the strength that was apparent from the beginning— so great!*

BIO:

My name is Aleena. I'm in 11th grade at Charlottesville High school. I'm originally from Afghanistan. I've been to United States of America for two years.

That Which Is Lost, Then Reclaimed
Mary Anderson

I have come to the mountains in that sacred hour.
As the light is fading,
bathing the trees far above
in pools of gold.

I have come to meet my ghost.

He exists in the cries of my mother,
crouching,
like a frightened rabbit
under the cover of darkness.

He is there in the beads of blood
stinging,
against sweat-drenched skin
on a hot summer night.

He is there in the silence;
He is there in the fear;
He is there in my former helplessness.

If I could visit the boy,
I would hold him.
I would stroke his hair.
I would tell him,
I am sorry this pain has come to you.
Yet, I would not want to finish his story.
that one day,
many years from now then,
his scars would become those of many others.
That all the things which matter most,
he would lose.
That he would become the monster he most feared.

If I could return to the little girl,
I would hold her.

I would stroke her hair.
I would tell her this.
One day,
long from now,
you will have a fierce, inexorable strength.
All that tried to make you feel small.
All that tried to shatter you,
thin you to the most fragile and breakable thing,
it won't win.
It will be only a ghost
that fades all the more
as your light shines the brighter.
Your scars, in time, will be gone.

If I could speak with the man now,
I would tell him this.
Despite what you have done,
I have risen from the deep with fire and power
beyond anything of your comprehension.

I have been released.

I was not able to save myself then.

And yet,
that was then.

How our judges and readers responded...

This is a moving and poetic account of devastating pain, but eventual resurrection. I am so glad that you can now separate your present for your past. ♥ *Lyrical and comforting. Nicely written.* ♥ *The lilting beauty of this poem is in its natural imagery and imaginative portrayal of reconciliation with past experiences.* ♥ *The author weaves a world of fantasy filled with color and sense that is the protagonist's own vision of finding meaning in the past and creating a narrative of strength and hope to propel one forward into a better future.*

Challenge into Change

BIO:

Writing is my greatest passion as well as hiking and generally spending time in nature. I also love the visual arts. I was born and raised right here in the Blue Ridge mountains. I've entered this contest because my family and I are survivors of domestic violence. I am grateful for each day of growth and the beauty to be found in this world.

Finding Strength in Pain
Anna

I cannot explain the rawness of pain,
The strained, crying face shaking and screaming,
The way strong shoulders break into a hollow shell,
A cry for help,
I cannot explain the weakness in pain,
The sheer vulnerability,
The way it is masked with a simple 'I'm fine',
The way the muscles tense and relax as waves hit,
I cannot explain the endlessness of pain,
The constant, looming darkness,
The anchor in your stomach,
The light at the end of the tunnel never coming closer,
I cannot explain the strength in pain,
Picking yourself up off the ground,
Overcoming the seemingly never-ending struggle,
Breathing deeply and digging through the rubble to find yourself
once again.

How our judges and readers responded…

Lovely way to take a common metaphor—light at the end of the tunnel—and change it to make it uniquely your own. ♥ *Your repetition of the phrase "I cannot explain" gives the poem a very strong, powerful rhythm that echoes the message of affirmation at the end.*

BIO:

My name is Anna and I am 16 years old. Writing is my coping mechanism of choice. I believe our experiences in life and any emotion we feel affects our quality of life, future behavior, and attitude. How we let them affect us is a choice.

Challenge into Change

Second Chance

Anonymous

Summer 2008 brought one of the WORST days of my life! There I stood, in criminal court before a judge overwhelmed, nervous, confused & scared as all get out! As I stood in disbelief, I felt like my heart must have skipped several beats and then tried to jump straight out my chest. The judge, seemingly frustrated asked me for the 3rd time, what did I plea?

I replied guilty. The I switched to not guilty. Finally, I indecisively asked the judge if I could plea both not guilty and guilty at the same time? I didn't like his answer.

I scanned the courtroom. My eyes narrowed in on my Mom and Dad. I could see the disappointment & utter sadness in their eyes. The look on their faces alone was enough to make me shrink from existence. I was deeply disturbed by the fact that I'd put my parents in a position to see their only daughter standing in court and accused of a crime.

My offense was not that serious (misdemeanor) and I had never been in trouble before. But still, I had to ponder. How in the world had this happen to me? How did I, a law-abiding citizen, an upholder of moral righteousness, find myself in this precarious position?

TRUTH be told, it was due to Medication. I have a serious mental illness and I'd stopped taking my psychiatric medication weeks earlier. As a direct result my behavior had become irrational, impulsive, paranoid & unpredictable.

I was appointed a lawyer. After hearing my story and obtaining my medical records, my lawyer advised me to plea Not Guilty by Reason of Insanity. I told her 1 would NEVER agree to that. NEVER! We eventually came up with another agreement.. My lawyer was able to get the Prosecution to agree to drop the charge against me, after explaining my story.

After court my lawyer gave me big hug. When we got outside the courtroom, she asked me PROMISE her that I would never stop taking my meds again. She told me I'd been given SECOND chance. I promised!! I also promised myself I'd never do anything that would have my parents in court glazing @ me with helpless eyes, grief and heavy hearts

This account is not about beating a criminal charge. This is about second chances! This incident occurred over 8 years ago, yet each time I see on the news of a mentally ill person going to jail, my heart breaks, because I know that could've been me.

I decided to get trained as Mentor/Presenter through NAMI (National Alliance of Mental Illness). My point in doing this was to educate my Peers, on the importance of self-care & MEDS! I volunteer to lead classes & make presentations primarily because I don't want anyone else with mental illness to ever have to stand before judge like I once did. I use my SECOND chance in hopes of preventing FIRST offenses.

How our judges and readers responded…

Thank you for sharing this hard-won narrative of courage and perseverance. ♥ Your memory of your day in court is so sharp, so distinct, that your readers feel like they are actually there—beautifully written!

BIO:

Courageous, brave, strong, fierce, determined woman on a mission!

Challenge into Change

Survivor

Anonymous

I blame myself for being ill. It's stupid, irrational, but as I look at my body, slim and young I feel betrayed by it. I shouldn't be sick, the endless blood tests that come back negative are a testament of it. I should be well but I'm not.

My home is my world now that I've given up my job. A strangely isolated world that barely touches any outside reality. Each day becomes a fight to remember, as I lie in my bed gazing up at the ceiling fan that my pain and fatigue are not who I am yet it seems it seems that the world, which I watch from my computer screen, has passed me by. I see pictures of births, jobs, trips, weddings. My friends are living life and as for me, well I'm not really living, I'm just waiting, hoping, wishing for a miracle around the corner to set me free me from the aching pain that keeps dragging me down.

I would love an ending for my story that ends with the doctors finding a cure that would help me instead of classifying me with vague useless labels but I'm not in a fairy story and all I can do is keep going day by day. The only thing I can change is my attitude which is hard. It's easy to dull pain with despair. To say "Nothing matters" so I'm alright. "I don't matter" so it doesn't matter that all I want to do is curl up and cry.

My body is broken. My mind is broken. I am still beautiful, no wait I said that wrong, I am more beautiful for my brokenness. I am weak but yet I am strong. I am a survivor.

How our judges and readers responded...

It is interesting to read this piece as a sort of letter to yourself; you are learning how to have a conversation with your own consciousness, how to allow yourself to feel your very real pain. This story takes a powerful turn toward the end, when you write "no wait:" you are editing your own internal conversation; you are literally rewriting your story as you realize how much you have learned from your circumstances.

BIO:

The author is 22 years old. After finishing college she went to do an internship to be a preschool teacher, she had to give it up because of her health and is now searching for a diagnosis.

Womanessence

Anonymous

That which endures
Is what matters:
After the ruthless winds
And the sunless scorching
Of day's descent
Into Night's abyss
With the raging firestorm
Of shards hot and cold
Blowing across
The Face of the Soul
Leaving no trace
In its train
But this:
The sturdy substance
Of a Silent Self
Still intact
While suffered
Whole.

How our judges and readers responded…

Your use of line breaks is powerful. ♥ *The language of deprivation and physical hardship was intense and rich.* ♥ *You remind us that we always have a silent self, even when it seems that everything else fails. It is this self that will bring us renewal.*

Los Ángeles Ayudan
Otilia Arroyo

Mi nombre es Otilia Arroyo y voy a compartir con ustedes una de mis cuantas caídas y cómo pude levantarme. Todo empezó en el año 2005. En ese año quedé completamente sin trabajo; en el 2006 arrestaron a mi esposo y lo encarcelaron por 11 años. A causa de eso sola con mis dos hijos menores. También tuve que entregar la casa donde vivíamos porque pertenecía a la compañía donde trabajaba mi esposo. Honestamente les digo que no teníamos a donde ir. Un hermano de mi esposo en lugar de apoyarme, quiso pisotearme más de lo que yo ya estaba. Gracias a Dios, uno de mis hermanos me apoyó, y nos fuimos a vivir con él, yo y mis dos hijos. Lo que era el comedor de la casa de mi hermano se convirtió en nuestra habitación. Tan solo cabía la cama y un gavetero. Nuestra cama era tipo litera (tres niveles de cama). Estuvimos allí por cuatro años.

No fue fácil para mis hijos convivir con mi sobrina, y tampoco para mí con mi cuñada. De hecho para el mayor de mis hijos fue imposible llevarse con ella. Tuve que mandarlo a vivir con una tía de parte de su papa en Texas. El más pequeño se acopló, excepto con la comida. Las amistades que visitaban la casa se comían la comida y meriendas de mi niño. En ese entonces él tenía 9 años.

Yo le pedí a Dios en todo momento que me diera la oportunidad de tener mi propio espacio aunque fuese debajo de un árbol. Toqué y toqué puertas. Algunas ni siquiera se abrían, otras se abrían, pero no me escuchaban. Pero no me di por vencida seguí tocando hasta que un día se me abrió una puerta bien, bien grandota.

Llamé a United Way a la Sra. Martha Trujillo para informarme sobre renta de apartamentos. Ella me envió a una reunión sobre ayuda para personas de escasos recursos en necesidad de vivienda. Allí encontré dos grupos de ayuda y tomé una tarjetita de cada uno. Llamé a la primera organización, dejé mi nombre, y no me llamaron. Luego de un mes llamé a Piedmont Housing Alliance, y allí dejé mensaje a la

Sra. Jo Olson, quien enseguida me respondió invitándome a pasar por su oficina. Llenamos la aplicación y me la aprobaron, y con ella misma fuimos al banco para verificar el crédito y ver si era posible. Yo me preguntaba, ¿Quién me va a dar un préstamo? No me daban seguridad porque mis ingresos eran muy bajos. Ella me motivó explicándome el proceso. Pasó un año y medio para encontrar algo que encajara con mi capacidad de pago. La Sra. Catherine Potter fue un ángel para mí en ayudarme a obtener el préstamo. Y que creen? Dios me escuchó y ya tengo 6 años viviendo en mi casa. Salí del fango donde estaba y todo gracias a Dios y las personas que fueron ángeles para mí quienes me ayudaron a hacer mi sueño realidad.

Cómo respondieron nuestros jueces y lectores...

Esta es una historia llena de esperanza. ♥ *Después de tantos momentos difíciles en tu vida y gracias a tu perseverancia, fuiste capaz de conseguir lo que tanto soñabas: tu casa propia.* ♥ *Gracias por recordarnos que en nuestros momentos más difíciles siempre hay personas (o ángeles) dispuestos a ayudarnos.*
♥ *Sí, hay colinas y valles en la vida. Me impresiona cómo perseveró, buscó ayuda, y ahora puede vivir una vida independiente.*

Biografía:

Otilia nació en El Salvador, ella es housekeeper y se considera a sí misma como una mujer emprendedora quien disfruta mantenerse ocupada, considera los retos de la vida como oportunidades para dar lo mejor de sí misma y continuar con su aprendizaje. Dentro de sus actividades preferidas, está el ir al gimnasio y dar caminatas para disfrutar de los paisajes que regala la ciudad de Charlottesville. Es poseedora de una fuerza interna que le ayuda a salir adelante con la frente en alto.

When Angels Help
(English translation from Spanish)
Otilia Arroyo

My name is Otilia Arroyo and I am about to share with you one of my many falls and how was I able to get back on my feet. Everything started in 2005. I had lost my job and in 2006 my husband had been sent to jail and was sentenced to 11 years in prison. Due to these events I was left by myself with my two little kids. Later on, I was forced to leave the house we were living in as it belonged to the company my husband used to work for. Unfortunately, my brother in law tried to make things worse for us. Luckily one of my brothers stepped up and decided to help me so me and my children stayed with him. The dining room became our bedroom, it was small, there was only room for a bed and a small dresser, we stayed there for four years.

For my kids living with my niece was not easy, it was also difficult for me to live with my sister in law. In fact, I had to send my oldest son to live with my husband's aunt in Texas. My youngest son learned to adapt except for the food. Sometimes friends and guests would eat my son's food, he was only 9 years old.

I prayed to God every day to give me the opportunity to have my own space even if it was under a tree. I knocked on many doors, some would not even open, some would open but they would not listen to me. However, I did not give up and I kept on knocking until one day a great big door opened.

I called Mrs. Martha Trujillo at United Way to request information about apartments rentals. She kindly referred me to a meeting about a program that helped people in need of housing. There I found two helping organizations, and I took a business card from each one. I called the first organization, I left my name and number but they never called. After a month I called Piedmont Housing Alliance and I left a message for Mrs. Jo Olson who responded immediately and invited me to her office. We filled out an application and I was approved, she even accompanied me to the bank to apply for a loan. I kept asking myself "Who would loan me money with such a low income?" She motivated me and explained the whole process. It was not until a year and a half later that we found something suitable to my income. Mrs. Catherine Potter was an angel to me as she helped me obtain the loan and guess what? God listened to me. I have been living in my own house for 6 years now. I got out of the mud and I owe everything to God and to those people who acted like angels to me and helped me make my dream come true.

How our judges and readers responded...

This is a story full of hope. After so many difficult moments in your life and through your perseverance, you were able to get what you wanted for so long: your own house. ♥ *Thank you for reminding us that in our most difficult times there are always people (or angels) willing to help us.* ♥ *Yes, there are hills and valleys in a life. I am impressed at how you persevered, sought help, and now can live an independent life.*

BIO:

Otilia was born in El Salvador, she is a housekeeper and considers herself an enterprising woman who enjoys keeping herself occupied, considers the challenges of life as opportunities to give her best and improve herself through her learning journey. Among her favorite activities, are working out and taking walks to enjoy the landscapes of the city of Charlottesville. She possesses an internal force that helps her to get ahead of any challenge.

Failure
Beverly B.

A 'Failure' I've always considered myself:

I can't begin to recall the number of Part-time, Minimum-wage Jobs I haven't been able to complete (nor do I *want to remember* the number of psychiatric hospitalizations I have had!);

I have completed 4 Teaching Certificates in 4 of the states in which I've lived – However, as told to me by the Head of the El Ed Department at my *Alma Mater*, "I would never teach" – And, it's been true – I didn't/haven't, much (even though I spent 3 summers attending Summer School in order to obtain these Certifications.)

Later, in 4 different states, I've begun Graduate Work, in 4 different Departments, where I thought, I could 'Make a Difference'. But, none of these Programs were completed: I either moved, or was hospitalized, or, Both!

I am a Divorcee.

During my last hospitalization, (at Region 10's *Crisis Intervention Center*), I felt like such a Failure as a mother.

Last Sunday I learned that I am not included in the extensive Genealogy my paternal 1st Cousin has done, (which reminded me, neither was I included in the names & addresses of my maternal 1st Cousins.)

However, presently, my personal challenge, I've recently come to realize, is to 'Wish Well' the Many Persons who now are doing, (& have done), *What I have thought I wanted to do.*

So, Where does that leave me in this my 80th Year?! – This 'Age & Stage' of my Life? It's been said that Psychiatric Survivors Lose **25 Years** of Their Lives--- *'105'? I don't think that's I!!*

Challenge into Change

Also, last Sunday, in our newly refurbished church basement, we continued our **SOUL MATTERS** Curriculum Group Discussion – This month's theme: **"Creation"**. And, in the (11 pages!) of this printed material, there was A Lot of information about **"Failure"!** Young Entrepreneurs, I learned, *Were Including in their Resumes What They'd Learned Through Their Failures!* And, More – Much More…

During our talking about **"Creation"**, I finally remembered what I passionately *really* wanted when I was 20-years-old: To follow/*To BE* the Principles I'd read in **The ART OF LIVING**. Yet, ya know what?, *I don't recall a single word in its 'Admonition'!* Exciting, isn't it? And, Full of Possibilities.

> Therefore,
> 'I would Grateful be…'
> For my Present Life;
> For my Many Opportunities;
> For "All That Is Our Life…"*

*From *Singing the Living Tradition* #128

How our judges and readers responded…

The story begins in an emotionally dark place, and I am heartsick for your troubles. Yet still, I see the strength emerging – the fact that you completed four teaching certificates despite significant challenges. I read on, following you as you move through the darkness, determined, and latch onto the light. ♥ I love the part when you write how young people are including their "failures" on their resumes; it shows that your heart is still open. And by the end, you are seeing a life full of possibilities again. ♥ Bravo.

Tribute to My Mother
Rosemary Balister

I admired my mother Lily Victoria Mines for the way she rose to the challenge of bringing us up in WW2 Britain. She was far from her Australian family and evacuated with us to the country in 1939. We could not go to school but she arranged for me to have correspondence lessons with my Grandfather who had been a teacher. I had one to one tuition from an early age. When I was a Brownie she made lavender bags to take in for a sale. She had me enter an art contest in a paper and I won a book once for my efforts. Finally, a way was found for me to go to school. If I walked half a mile a man was willing to drive me with his son. She made me embroidered crochet mittens an on the walk I looked down at them thinking someone loved me. When we returned to London the bombing was still going on and our school took a direct hit but not while children were in it. My parents went round to the Head teacher who stood in tears amid the ruins of her school. She referred to them as "Towers of strength at an awful time." She was a Commonwealth citizen but with the other residents of England at that time helped the country live through its finest hour and defeat the evil of Naziism.

How our judges and readers responded…

A concise yet beautifully written tribute. ♥ *You convey your mother's small but significant acts of care wonderfully.* ♥ *I love that you express so much with so few words.*

Challenge into Change

BIO:

I was born in 1936 in London, England. I came to the USA in 1966. I have lived in Charlottesville since 1972. All three children graduated from CHS and the older two attended Jefferson School. I have a BA in German from Bristol University and their Graduate Certificate in Education. I taught at the City of Worcester Grammar School for Girls, 1957 – 1959, and at Sunbury Grammar School 1959 – 1960. I also taught ESL at the SW Herts College of Further Education. I married Michael Balister in 1959.

Untitled

Rachael Ballard

Sometimes I miss having a dad

But what he did was bad

I won't tell you his crime

But sooner or later I will run out of time

One day he is going to be free

What if he comes back for me?

If I grow to be twenty I will be brave

If I'm too brave I might end up digging his grave

But what he did was wrong

I won't tell you how long

But he's going to be out there

One day what he might do will be no dare

What if no one helps me?

Then I won't be free

Then I think he won't get me, he will never get me

How our judges and readers responded…

The rhyming of the piece gives each line a pleasurable musicality that is fascinating because it runs somewhat counter to the more frightening subject matter. ♥ *I want to know more about what dad did, but the author's declaration "I won't tell you his crime" lets me know that it is not information that I should have.* ♥ *The language is quiet in its feeling, never letting on just how deeply engraved on the author the "crime" is but informing us just enough to know that the desire to be "free" speaks volumes.*

Challenge into Change

Where I'm From
Rebecca Ballard

I'm from the echoing tap from the claws on the floor
And her so very cute howl that brightens my day everyday

I'm from the smell of my mom's freshly cooked brownies
And the memorable smell of my great grandmother's house

I'm from 6 years-worth of the swoosh of the net
And barking and smiling joy from the hounds

I'm from chocolate goodness at the donut place
And from Taco Bell and movies with friends

I'm from the wild wild West
Then suddenly from the historical east

I'm from the people that save from disaster
Cameron, Ryan, and Rachael

I'm from the park and the swinging of lyrics
And my room the place where I can finally cry from emotional hurt

I am from memories of abuse and memories of a family who once
used to be a family

I am from future dreams that one hopes comes true

How our judges and readers responded...

This piece is so elegant. ♥ *There is a strength in the use of language as it moves slowly from unfamiliarly descriptive, such as "the claws on the floor...her so very cute howl" to extremely familiar "Taco Bell", "wild wild West".* ♥ *It is rare to encounter a piece that makes me feel so close to the author yet also such an extreme and unbridgeable distance that I'm desperate to decrease.*

My Life Story
Irene Barbera

I came from Africa. My country is Democratic Republic of Congo. I want to share with you my life story.

I was born in October 20, 1992. I was the first born. I didn't have the chance the live with my family because of the war. My dad died when I was little, around four years old. I never remember his face. They just showed me his picture. He left only me. My mom decided to get another husband. She left me with my grandfather.

I grew up with my Aunt's family. She paid my school fees for primary school and secondary school (high school).

When I finished high school; we went to live in Uganda/Kampala because our life situation was so bad. We went there like refugees. Life was still bad because it was difficult to find the good life. But God makes the way, and we came to the United States.

My life is changed now. I can buy the shelter I want. I continue to learn English now to improve my skills. That is a good step for me. I thank God everything He did in my life.

How our judges and readers responded...

Your voice comes through this story very strongly, even though you don't tell a lot of details. That spare quality makes it beautiful, and also makes me want to know more about your life. ♥ The line, "They just showed me his picture" communicates so much about your relationship to your father and your family; it's a strong way to say how much you missed out on by not being able to have more time with your father. ♥ I am so glad you are in America. I hope your future will be bright here.

I Am the Face
Allison Barnes

I am the face

Do you see me?

Do you care about me?

Do you love me?

I am the face

Sometimes I become very good at appearing happy and smile. Although a lot of the times im dying inside.

Inside my heart hurts, I cry

And there are times I have wanted to die

But thank the lord, and Jesus above who showed me so much love.

I live to fight my demons inside. Everyday life is a battle that I have to face. And I still try to fight then with a smile grace, and be blessed throughout the day. However, the demons inside makes me feel that I am unworthy of love.

Do you see my face, do you hear my countless times I've asked for help?

Sometimes even if someone says hi instead of a goodbye. Or if someone even asks me how I'm doing it gives me the strength to get by.

Do you see my face?

The demons that I fight every day is called mental illness(s). I didn't choose mental illness. However, just because I have them, I still continue to fight, and do what is right. And just because I and other people in the world have mental illness doesn't mean that we are not smart, or dumb. We are still everyday people, that will continue to excel in our abilities instead of our disabilities. With my mental illness I have accomplished so much and it was sent from Jesus, God and other people with so much love. I have successfully achieved 1 certificates, a diploma, my associates college degree.

I'm telling anyone to continue to fight, to live, and not let the demons consume me (us). Even in our darkest hours we must believe, love, honor, cherish ourselves, even if no one does.

Because I am the face of mental illness.

How our judges and readers responded…

This poem stands as a declaration of humanity that refuses to be invisible. ♥ *The series of questions establishes an insistence that drew me deeper into the essay to learn of your struggles. And then, as you name your "demons inside" as mental illness, your tone shifts to one of courage and accomplishment, even calling on others with mental illness to "believe, love, honor, cherish ourselves."* ♥ *I was deeply moved by your dedication of your poem to your cousin. Coping with mental illness is a great challenge.* ♥ *Your poem is a statement of pain and hope and achievement.*

BIO:

I wrote this poem to bring awareness of mental illness. Lift the individuals who have them to continue to fight, and try do what is right. And lastly to honor, love, cherish to my cousin who committed suicide in 2015.

Some Women
Frances Curtis Barnhart

Some women
Walk through walls at night.

Some lie awake
Afraid to toss or turn
All frozen into silence.

Some women hold
Pillows against their eyes, against the dark
Against their ears and mouths
And all the portals
Where childhood memories are stored.

Some hold their pillows tight against the night
And fear to let them go when it turns light.

Some women wear tailored suits
Spike heels, walk briskly
Bravely into day
Making names for themselves
And at night handle razor blades
To make the blood flow
Proving there is life beneath the skin

Some can't be with others or by themselves
Some step only on the brightest stones
Daring not to peek into the dark
Wells that are the archives of themselves.

Some women tremble with each sound they hear
Tripping over obstacles of grief or fear.

Some women reflect the red and orange of the night
They walk through caves of fire and burn bright
Some of these are the same women, one leading another into solace,
Some are magical alchemists,

Challenge into Change

Turning leaden memories to gold.

Some of us are the same women.
We eat our dreams like medicine
Or fresh sweet melons
Depending on the night, depending on the mood
And when the panic's past, the sorrow
We keep our lives moving along
Praying it is only our best
We are expected to do.

We reside here in holy love for one another,
Knowing what we have in common with each other.

We have swallowed, alternately, periodically,
Bits of broken glass
But we have also tasted the sweet juices
Of sun ripe mangos as
We dine at the table of time.

We are the women,
Rooted in the earth the way we are
Touching with our fingertips, the heavens,
Caressing with our palms, the sky
Smoothing sweet salve over our skin
Reaching each other with our song
Longing to know where we belong
For we are the warriors,
The healers, the poets
And together out of compassion and love
We are the feminine face of God.

How our judges and readers responded...

*Through images of eating and sleeping, this poem contrasts the interior feelings of
pain with its exterior expression.* ♥ *When "some women" are revealed to be
the same women, the poem envisions a feminine community even as it suggests
personal and sometimes isolating challenges.*

BIO:

Frances Curtis Barnhart is a mother of three, grandmother of ten, spiritual explorer and an evolutionary activist in the human potential movement. Her new book The Beauty of Impermanence: A Woman's Memoir is available from Amazon. She is a poet and author of The New Woman Warrior's Handbook: Not for Women Only [Illuminated Way Press, 1982 and has appeared in MS Magazine, The New York Times Magazine and Artemis,. Barnhart remarried at seventy and now lives in Roanoke, VA

Dios Te Bendiga y Te Llene de Victoria
Liliana Bedoya

Cuando mi vida se inundó con la alegría de saber que estaba esperando a mi primer hijo, decidí darles la noticia a mis padres, sin embargo poco tarde en descubrir que ellos no compartían mi emoción. La reacción inmediata de mi padre fue echarme de su casa, por lo que tuve que buscar refugio donde fuese, pues ya no era sólo yo a quien tenía que cuidar, sino al hijo que estaba esperando.

La situación no fue más fácil después del parto. Una mañana al despertar, descubro que no hay nada para comer, ni para alimentar a mi hijo, por lo que decido ir a la tienda y pedir leche fiada, sin embargo al no tener manera de pagar, me lleno siento avergonzada; sé que no debo seguir poniendo a mi hijo en esta situación, y al ver su rostro de felicidad de por haber comido, obtengo la fuerza para tomar una decisión que cambiaría nuestras vidas.

Decidí, junto con dos amigas, migrar hacia los Estados Unidos, mi cabeza se llena de un puñado de ilusiones, pero mi cuerpo refleja miedo y valentía al mismo tiempo. Una vez que llego a la frontera con México, mis amigas deciden regresar, de nueva cuenta es momento de continuar sola el camino. Me siento a observar para aprender un poco sobre la cultura mexicana, y poder adoptarla con el afán de pasar desapercibida por la policía y autoridades migratorias, así es como logro llegar hasta la frontera con Estados Unidos. Una vez ahí, decido contactar a mi familia para solicitar su apoyo y lograr mi cometido, sin embargo su respuesta fue la misma que cuando les dije que estaba embarazada: me dieron la espalda.

Impulsada por la bendición de Dios y el amor a mi hijo, logro llegar al estado de Nueva York donde se encuentran familiares que me brindan un espacio para vivir y comenzar a trabajar como niñera, sin embargo esto no duraría mucho, pues al poco tiempo deciden regresar a Guatemala. Ahora me encuentro esperando a mi segundo hijo, y sin un lugar seguro para vivir, emprendo el viaje hacia donde el dinero me alcance.

Con mi fe en todo lo alto, llego al filo de la medianoche a Richmond, VA, camino con mis hijos entre la oscuridad, y como por obra divina, al final de la calle hay una luz iluminando un seminario, al tocar la puerta, no imaginaba que estaría a punto de ser bendecida nuevamente, pues una de las personas del seminario me abriría las puertas de su casa por un año, dándome la oportunidad de enfocarme en hacer algo productivo para mí y mi familia. Al pasar del tiempo, con un nivel de inglés básico, me gradúo como cosmetóloga, ejerciendo de primera instancia al visitar a mis clientas en sus casas, y posteriormente inauguro uno de los primeros salones de belleza hispanos de la ciudad. Todo gracias a la bendición de Dios.

Cómo respondieron nuestros jueces y lectores…

Tu ensayo me recuerda al dicho "La fe mueve montañas." Tu fe y el inmenso amor a tu hijo hacen tu historia fascinante. ♥ *¡Felicitaciones por todos tus logros!* ♥ *Tu realmente luchaste para lograr el éxito que soñabas. La ayuda de otra persona y la fe en Dios hicieron toda la diferencia.*

Biografía:

Liliana nació en El Salvador, desde muy joven entendió el valor del trabajo duro y cómo ella es artífice de su propio destino. Se considera como una mujer que ha enfrentado una gran cantidad de retos, pero ha logrado salir adelante gracias a su fe y a las bendiciones que Dios ha derramado sobre su vida, sabedora de esto, brinda apoyo a todas aquellas personas que se acercan a ella con el objetivo de ayudarlas a desarrollar todo su potencial. Ella es una mujer con una gran motivación por salir adelante, y quien busca dejar un legado positivo en todos aquellos quienes la conocen, pero sobre todo en su familia.

God Blesses You and Fills You with Victories
(English translation from Spanish)
Liliana Bedoya

When my life was filled with the joy of knowing I was pregnant, I decided to share the news with my parents, but they did not share my happiness. On the contrary, my father's immediate reaction was to kick me out of his house, so I had to seek shelter wherever I could, because it was not only myself anymore, now I had someone else to take care of.

My situation wasn't easy after my son was born. One morning when I woke up, I found out that I had no food and was unable to feed my son, so I decided to go to the store and beg people for milk, having no way to pay made me feel ashamed; I was conscious that I could not continue to put my son through this, and after seeing the happiness in his face after having eaten I got the strength I needed to make a life changing decision for the two of us.

Along with two other friends, I decided to migrate to the United States, my head was filled with hope, but my body reflected fear and courage at the same time. Once I arrived at the Mexican border, my friends decided to go back; but I decided to continue this adventure by myself. I tried to learn the Mexican culture, in order to be able to adopt it and go unnoticed by the police and immigration authorities; this is how I managed to reach the US border. Once there, I contacted my family to ask for their support so I could achieve my mission, however their response was the same as when I told them I was pregnant: they turned their backs on me.

Guided by God's blessing and the love for my son, I managed to arrive in the state of New York where some relatives provided me with a place to stay and I started working as a babysitter; this would not last too much as I decided to go back to Guatemala. Later on, I found myself pregnant with my second child, but no place to live so I decided to start traveling until I ran out of money.

With my faith at the highest, I managed to arrive in Richmond, VA at midnight. I walked with my children through the dark streets, and suddenly as if it was a miracle I saw a Seminary at the end of the street. I knocked on the door and at that point I couldn´t imagine how blessed I was about to be. A person from the Seminary offered me to be her guest for a whole year, thus giving me the opportunity to focus on achieving something productive for me and my family. Time went by and even with my basic understanding of English I was able to graduate as a cosmetologist; I first worked by visiting clients at their homes, and later in time by opening one of the first Hispanic beauty salons in the city. All thanks to God's blessing.

How our judges and readers responded...

Your essay reminds me of the saying "Faith moves mountains." Your faith and immense love for your son make your story fascinating. ♥ *Congratulations on all your achievements!* ♥ *You truly struggled to achieve the success you dreamt of. The help of another person and faith in God made all the difference.*

BIO:

Liliana was born in El Salvador, since a very young age she understood the value of being a hard worker and how she is the architect of her own destiny. She considers herself a woman who has faced a great number of challenges, but has managed to get ahead of them thanks to her faith and the blessings that God has poured out on her life, therefore, she supports all those who approach her to realize their full potential. She is a woman with a great motivation to improve herself, and who seeks to leave a positive legacy in all those who know her, but especially in her family.

Day by Day by
Elle M. Bergert

My friend's basement has windows facing the woods, and has grown home-like in my seven months here. The makeshift kitchenette, complete with coffee grinder, and living room/bedroom combo is warmed by electric "burning logs." I convince myself it has the luxuries of a real home, aided by the smell of fresh brewed coffee, a little deck and the cherished woods. Watching deer and hearing bird songs soothe me. But mostly, I am just so grateful that I feel safe.

He had a rough 'n tumble, masculine image even his name implied. A thick head of white hair and mustache, he was compared, often, to Sam Elliot, and the voice, also like Sam, deep and sultry. But the polish and money of a Hollywood cowboy was not part of this package. Rough edges from an unresolved, extremely poor and abusive childhood, my handsome man was unstable. A very tender side diverted from the underlying volatility for a while. My cat loved to curl up in his lap to be stroked. At his most tender, he loved to comb my very ordinary hair. I recall him patiently crawling on the floor with my toddler grandson, in search of the kitty. He cheerfully did household repairs and mowed the grass,

With time, his good intentions and "love" were eclipsed by threatening behavior, verbal and physical, more aggressive with his growing insecurity. Sexual demands warped familiar pattern of intimacy into something not playful, loving or safe. For months I struggled in fear, trying to say, "It's over." Then one day, in rage, he stormed out the kitchen door, vowing never to return. I shook as I locked the deadbolt. He would be back within hours, pounding on that door. But I absolutely knew, I would never again unlock that door to him. Threats soon followed, both shocking and criminal. I was terrified. He analyzed every piece of information he had about me, to find ways to use it against me and evoke fear. He wanted to destroy me and I began to feel he might succeed. I tried to navigate the legal system for protection, but it was dehumanizing and fruitless in the end.

My beloved home now has renters. Most belongings are in storage. I changed my car, my phone, my address, my license plates and my town. Domestic abuse was shameful for me to call by name. It was hard to identify when the abuse began and in the end, to forgive myself for "letting" it happen. I knew when I bolted that door; my life was going to get much worse before it got better. I wasn't yet prepared to lose my home and all my security. Recovery is taking time, courage, a network of kindness and hardest of all, my willingness to begin again. Some days, I remember, fear grabs me and tears flow. This morning, as I sipped my coffee, I noticed that I was feeling hopeful, even optimistic. I am thankful. And apparently stronger, day by day.

How our judges and readers responded...

Domestic abuse is a terrible problem, yet you had the strength to overcome it. ♥
Some very strong writing, and compelling contrasts between gentle and violent aspects of some relationships. Most persuasive line: "I changed my car, my phone, my address, my license plates and my town." Conveys recovery which isn't yet complete...I come away from this essay optimistic that this writer will remain steadfast and confident that she's on her way to a saner, safer life. ♥ *The writer shows that oftentimes domestic abuse follows what starts out as seemingly beautiful times. Hence the difficulty to leave once the abuse begins because so many good things and good times have been shared.* ♥ *The careful, exact phrasing of each sentence in this piece takes the reader through a range of experiences, from gentle moments of peace to terrifying times of persecution. In the end, the author achieves a portrait of a life on the mend, drawing strength to begin anew amid the sorrow of the past.*

Challenge into Change

BIO:

I am a mother and a grandmother. All my life, I have wanted to be recognized as a writer. Years ago, I served as Associate Director of Publications at a university and that was as close as I came to a writing career. But my real passion was to complete and sell a screenplay. That piece of writing has been sitting, half finished, for several years. Hopefully, this writing exercise encourages me to finish my screenplay and realize my dream.

Blossom in Wood

Joncey Boggs

Planted, roots stretching dutifully down into soil
Carefully spaced in a tidy garden row,
My blossom striving to look just like yours, only bigger.

The spade rips at earth to divide,
Earth, rock, and me dumped in the corner of the yard,
Where nothing is the same.

I do not know you blade and branch and twisted roots,
I do not know you shadow and shade,
Interrupting my open sky.

But here I see what wasn't there before,
Light reaching through woods, all honeyed and diamond touched,
Giving form to the different.

And I am part of blades and branches and roots that move,
Meeting the light in all the cracks,
Blooming now because I am.

How our judges and readers responded...

I love the repetition of "blades and branches and roots;" the phrase has a wonderful rhythm and by repeating it you show so clearly the shift in perspective between the first moment and the second. ♥ *The description of the light as "honeyed and diamond touched" is the most beautiful moment of the poem.* ♥ *Your poem is a beautiful reminder that we can thrive not only in a garden, but also in the woods. Life finds a way.*

Challenge into Change

BIO:

Joncey Boggs is a Charlottesville native. She works as the Outreach Coordinator for On Our Own of Charlottesville and has directed several local theater productions. Joncey has raised four children in Charlottesville and eagerly awaits grandchildren.

Divorce Laugh to Keep from Crying
Sheila Boling

Sometimes when you go through a divorce you just have to laugh to keep from crying.

When you get married to stand before God, family, friends and you vow to be with that person until death do you part. You say I do and things are going well. Then suddenly the things that brought you together are the very things that tear you apart. No matter how you tried to stay together you just can't get past things that were done or said in anger. You may realize you are not compatible at all.

So you separate for 3 months or 1 year depending on your assets or if you have children, etc. During this time you try to put the pieces back together. You look at yourself and reflect on things that went wrong. You think about the things that your spouse/partner complained about can be changed. You decide if you can make the changes without changing who you are as a person. You even try counseling because in all honesty no one wants their marriage to end. You meet and try to work things out. However, you realize that you can't work out the issues. More things are done or said to make it in impossible.

Now here is where the three stages of divorce come in the good the bad and the ugly.

Stage 1: The hurt that your marriage failed and you are getting a divorce. You have to listen to what people are saying. The typical things I'm sorry it didn't work out. Oh what happened? The favorite he or she wasn't the right person for you but I didn't want to hurt you. You looked so happy. You cry and cry some more because it didn't work out.

Stage 2: The anger and rage because it has ended. You are mad because of the mean and hurtful comments. You are mad because people keep running to tell you that they saw him or her and they were with someone. You are mad because when the holidays come around you think about the engagement or the marriage. You reflect on the goods times because it was not all bad. Then you are even madder. At times you are mad when any man or woman even tries to talk to you. You chew them out and spit them out. Then you laugh because otherwise you will be crying.

Stage 3: Moving on... The ink on the divorce papers have dried. You are done with the hurt, anger, rage and tears. You do things that make you happy. You regain your confidence that you lost. You regain your self-esteem. You realize you are better than you give yourself credit for. You look back and you just laugh at what you did or the way you acted. You are no longer the deranged divorcee. You pick up the pieces and you move on. You ready to go on with your life. You have moved on when you want your ex to be happy and meet someone. You have moved on when you know you may not have been the right person for them.

People think that women should wear divorce on their forehead like a badge of honor especially if you have been married more than once. They will say third time a charm, haha. So you smile and say you never know. They repeat themselves and you smile and say the same thing. You really want to say something mean. You laugh to keep from crying. You have moved on when you open your heart up to new adventures, new people, and new desires.

So don't think of divorce as a bad word.

Define - Don't let divorce define who you are as a person

Independent - Newfound independence

Vibrant - Vow to be you, vow to change if it brings out the best in you

Opportunities - The opportunities are endless

Romance - Romance will come your way when you open your heart

Courage - The courage to move beyond divorce, rage, hurt, tears. The confidence in knowing you beat the label tattooed on your forehead

Enjoy- Enjoy everything that life has to offer, **E**mpowered to move forward

Divorce laugh to keep from crying

How our judges and readers responded…

You have come through the trauma of divorce and are now on the other side. Your story will speak to so many. There is encouragement here for women considering, or currently going through, a divorce. ♥ *The DIVORCE acronym helped to pull the author's writing together, taking a word that can include much hurt and sorrow and using positive, uplifting words to define it.* ♥ *In this piece, the author reflects on the challenges of divorce and the stages by which one may overcome these.* ♥ *The prose moves confidently and powerfully, taking the reader vicariously on a journey of frustration, despair, and into redemption and confidence.*

BIO:

I live in Covesville, VA and was a twin. I lost her to breast cancer so I run the Women's Four Miler because of her. I enjoy running, gardening and gathering with friends and family.

Challenge into Change

Spirit of Being Me
Katherine A. Borges

I find great inspiration writing in the wee hours of the night from my personal angels. You may not know you have angels around you, but you do. Even those that have crossed over are with you whether you call them or not. This may seem crazy to you, so be it. It's my page and I don't care what anybody says or thinks of me. All I know is the truth and the truth is all you will ever get from me. I can live and die with that. God or whomever you consider a higher being in your life is my witness.

We come from different places, have done different things. We have faced ups and downs and continue to plow through the challenges or surprises in our lives. While some complain, some of us rejoice of wonderful things that have happened in our lives. We are different flavors and not one of us 'taste' the same. To me, this is the beauty and reality in our world. While some folks attain the 'good life' early, there are those of us still struggling living paycheck to paycheck just to get by. I gather my experience in a 'medicine bag' and pull out this experience when I want to, as long as I am true to my SELF. Being unique comes to mind.

I don't ask 'why' so much as I did as a child. I try not to complicate my life. I feel keeping life situations simple. Simple works for me, does it for you? Have you tried?

Do we REALLY have to wait for a near-death experience, to know all life is beautiful? To some of us, it has. Are we so caught up with one another's trials and tribulations we forget about our own life? Have we REALLY shared our joys and not think or feel another's joy to be vain or egotistical? I say not, but others do.

We are not perfect. I do not like the word and have excluded the word from my vocabulary. To me, it doesn't exist. I accept you, just the way you are. I don't see imperfection, because I accept you, just the way you are.

I refuse to judge. I have a problem with that too. Like the saying, live and let live, just mind your own business.

You can strip me of my worldly possessions. The few possessions I have, have given away because I don't need them anymore. Though what you can never have is my spirit for living. That is mine and I do what I please with it and I hope you do too.

So by chance, you are perplexed to why I am writing this. It's because I love you. Even if I don't know you and if I do, you know I do love you. No, I'm not dying. I'm just living. It's just the spirit of being me.

How our judges and readers responded...

I love the line "it's my page and I don't care what anybody says"—I think "it's my page" is such a strong and beautiful way to describe what it means to be a writer, to claim a place in the world, and to speak your piece. ♥ *The metaphor of the "medicine bag" is a wonderful one for describing the way one can draw on one's experience through life.* ♥ *You have an inspiring attitude toward yourself, toward others, toward life.* ♥ *You have learned a lot by living. Thank you for sharing.*

Challenge into Change

BIO:

Katherine is a Breast Cancer survivor resident in the City of Charlottesville, Virginia. She has self-published Two Collections of Poetry: Bare Tree and Naked Leaves. Also a Collection of Photos: Images of Albemarle County. Katherine is currently working on a third Collection of poetry and a picture book of Charlottesville, both to be self - published in 2017. She is a blog writer, photographer and her work can be seen in Blogger and Google+. Contact:. Kat955@gmail.com.

Pilgrimage
Brittany

I spent most of 2009 walking up and down hills with 35 pounds strapped to my back. The Appalachian Trail, a 2000-mile mountain trail up the east coast, had captured my imagination and that of thousands of other wannabe thru-hikers. Driven by the idea of a pilgrimage through nature, I had committed myself to the whole six-month journey of "walking with spring" from Georgia to Maine. It was not to be.

I quickly fell in with a group of tattooed crust punks carrying heavy canvas survivalist gear and six-packs of watery beer. When we laid down our heads at night on the damp leaves, we filled the quiet spaces between us with talk of feminism, homelessness, and American overconsumption. By day we learned how to bake biscuits over flat stones, how to listen for running water, how to read the sky for signs of rain. When we hitchhiked to a town to restock, we filled up on cake icing and enough toilet paper for another five days. We lived in the present, without concern for the onward march of the seasons. Unfortunately, when it snowed on me in October, I couldn't handle it. I was cold. I was also heartbroken. My pilgrimage was a failure. I rested four days in an appropriately symbolic yellow wood - Robert Frost would have liked it - and there my path diverged. The next day I hiked out to the nearest road and cried.

I stuck out my thumb and hitchhiked to a commune in Virginia. It was 450 acres of farm and pasture, woods and water, and an unobstructed sky. It was a balm to a heart ripped too soon from the mountains, and it gave me a place to recover. By day, my hands were in the earth, clearing weeds from next spring's asparagus and harvesting sweet fall carrots. By night, I thanked the trees for the blessing of dry wood crackling in the stove that warmed the visitor cabin. And while the land held me, it also invited me to make a temporary home. So I worked alongside the residents as they milked the cows, fixed the cars, changed the diapers, mourned the dead, and looked after every

Challenge into Change   61

aspect of life in what amounted to a small village. When we sat down to dinner together, chipped plates overflowing with meat and vegetables and warm yeast bread of our own making, I saw people genuinely glad and thriving on a simple life. This was enough. My campfire conversations had led me here. Question was, did I want to take the next step?

Yes, I did. I moved in not long after.

It is the cold season again. We have sown cover crop of oats and unrolled hay mulch to put the garden to bed for the winter. My own bed is piled high with quilts against the ticklish drafts of this rustic bedroom. Putting down roots, I have never felt so solid as I do here. My pilgrimage took me here, at last.

How our judges and readers responded...

You have a lovely voice, idiosyncratic and interesting. ♥ *I especially love the moment when you say that "Robert Frost would have liked it"; you convey your own frustration with yourself and the situation, as well as making clear the beauty of the world around you.* ♥ *You have discovered that life in a community where a garden is tended, not life in nature, is your source of sustenance.*

BIO:

Brittany lives at Twin Oaks Community, organizes the yearly Twin Oaks Women's Gathering, and grows vegetables.

A New Me
Brenda Brown-Grooms

Labor Day, 1998, I was 43, and in my first pastorate. My community consisted of Deacons and Deaconesses and choir and church members, who lived in my hollow, or the hollows surrounding mine.

Henry Pippen my huge, black, adolescent lab/chow, who had flunked obedience school, because he had no manners, didn't like many people. The feeling was mutual.

We headed out for a walk. I felt wobbly, so we skipped going up the hill to the church. I had a month long, worse "flu" EVER. Later, I went to a picnic. My insides felt like jello. I came home early, fed Pippen, let him out to "do his business," and went to bed.

The next morning, I called the nearest ER. "If you don't feel better, you should come to the hospital." I decided to wash dishes, so I could think. I had trouble holding plates, and could not lift pots. A nagging suspicion was growing in the pit of my stomach. I went to brush my teeth. The right side of my face was numb. Then, I knew. I'd had a stroke. It was at least 16 hours since my knees buckled. Too late to use the clot busting t-PA (tissue plasminogan activator) to minimize the damage -- and that was only a viable option if my stroke was caused by a clot, and not a bleed. I called my neighbor Deaconess to drive me to hospital. She fussed. I cried. She cried. I did not yet know that I was never meant to do all the ministry of a church.

"I think I've had a stroke," I told a nurse. I had. There were no neurologists at that hospital, but I didn't have the energy to be transferred. I made the decision to stay the night, for I knew, there was now no way to mitigate any damage to my brain. I kept trying to move during the night. It became more and more difficult. I want to move my bowels. I couldn't.

Mama and Aunt Phee came the next day. I dragged to a chair to eat. I could not swallow on the right side of my mouth. When I tried to get up from the chair, I could no longer walk. I could speak a little louder than a whisper. Nothing on the right side of my body worked! I am a preacher, a singer! How could I live with half a body? Who would care for ill-mannered Pippen? What would happen to the church?

In those moments, I experienced the deepest fear I'd ever known. Then, a comforting warmth flowed over me. I didn't know how I'd be alright, or what a new me would look like. I did know that the old me was gone. She died Labor Day, 1998.

Now I am a different me. And, just as God promised me, sitting in a chair that I couldn't get myself out of, I am neither dead nor a vegetable.

How our judges and readers responded...

A remarkable story, told powerfully. With language spare and unsentimental, you take us on your journey of having a stroke. ♥ In my mind's eye, I see a woman who, though frightened and alone, faces the reality of what is happening to her with fortitude and matter-of-factness. And humor — goodness, such a wry wit, and such tenderness toward your dear dog! I daresay these qualities helped you through the ordeal as much as anything. And in the end, you blossom anew. ♥ I am glad that there is a new you after a stroke, and that you know that this new you is still you! ♥ People need to hear your message.

BIO:

Brenda Brown-Grooms is Co-Pastor of New Beginnings Christian Community, in Charlottesville, VA, her home town. She is also a Performance Artist, a Singer, a Writer, and a Professional Story Teller.

Loving You! The Day of Sunshine!
Patricia Burley-Choloski

The wind was blowing, a cool breeze. There are signs of spring, the sun warming to feel. There is an increase in outdoor activities as people are jogging and spending time in nature. It feels great to spend time in nature as it gives you a new outlook on life. Being in nature also provides a connection like nothing else. It's the glowing feeling that really suits you. Take it for all it's worth, it's a wonderful gift. Thank God for all his wonderful gifts. As we look upon what's next in our life, why not be mindful of what's going on now. It makes more sense to connect with the present moment. See how it feels to think about the right now. How does that make you feel? Do you feel connected, grounded? As we grow, there are great learning experiences all around us. We can thank God, our heavenly father for our parents, siblings and relationships with ourselves and others. What would happen if we did not have all those wonderful people in our lives? It's a blessing to have yourself and others. How you treat yourself is how others will treat you. It's amazing what a shift in our thinking can do. Do you look upon others to make you happy? Is there a need to be validated by others to feel human? Can I go out into the world and validate myself? How does it feel having a relationship with yourself? What if you become comfortable with yourself, how would that improve you responding to yourself? What if you become comfortable with yourself, how would that improve you responding to yourself? Would you respect yourself more and know you can and should love yourself? Could you wake up in the morning and still have respect for yourself? Give yourself praise and understanding on a daily basis. Recognize you are important to yourself. Give honor and glory to God!

As I walk upon a shadow I feel its warmth embracing you. To love you is to honor yourself. To respect you is to recognize yourself. To feel you is to acknowledge yourself.

Will you ever be the same again as you climb that ladder and embrace yourself?

Loving you,

Your sister,

Pat Burley-Choloski

How our judges and readers responded...

Reading your piece feels like meditating. ♥ *It provides the same kind of serenity, the same feeling of calmness.* ♥ *A great reminder to get back in touch with nature as a generative means of self-discovery.*

A Family Legacy
Debbie Calabretta

Dedicated to:
My Parents, Grandparents, JC, AH, JP-T, and IR
With your love, support, strength, guidance and inspiration all things are
possible.

We travel many roads in a lifetime. Sometimes we find ourselves on a dark and isolated road filled with loneliness. I was raised in a family with much love, deep roots and strong values. Family members always helped each other in times of joy and sorrow. It was instilled in me from a young age, to depend upon the family's strength, courage, perseverance and faith.

It was a day of celebration with family and friends until the monster stepped out of the darkness with a gun. The monster threatened my family with severe harm, then chose to end its own life instead. To witness this act was horrific. As days pass the aftermath was disabling. Thinking? Focusing? These all became chores. Fear of everyone and everything was constant. The angry monster penetrated and consumed every ounce of energy. Getting out of bed, going to work was a struggle. Daily chores became a burden, my own home became a prison.

So many question's; How could I allow this monster into my life and cause such pain? Who was I and what have I become? Why am I imprisoned in deep darkness? This is not me. Where is my happy family?

Through intense soul searching, I realized my family's legacy is what I needed to depend upon. Although some days are still a struggle, the glimmer of light has peered through the darkness.

Challenge into Change

It is the light of God's Grace and warm embrace that allows me to fly in freedom; put the monster to rest and leads me to know "I am OK".

How our judges and readers responded...

"The word "monster" has such a power in this piece and says so much about the harm that the author and family suffered as a result of the monster's deeds. ♥ *I especially love this line: "The angry monster penetrated and consumed every ounce of energy." A "monster" is a character that could sound like something from a children's book, but here it is clearly a source of fear, loss, and anguish.* ♥ *The essay flows so nicely that it feels as if I, the reader, am there to witness the events, as if I am traveling with the author as they experience them."*

BIO:

I live in Scottsville, VA with my husband and our pet Shetland Sheepdog. We have two adult children and two precious Grandchildren. My hobbies include spending time with my family, reading, hiking, travel and relaxing on the beach.

Grand Mothers
Monique Collins Carey

My Grandmothers are the epitome of grand, dignified, royal, not easily broken, as if possessing super powers. They've endured more than I know, but remain forever strong, beautiful, and revered by me. My paternal Grandmother, Maggie is over 90 years old today. She has lived to see the first African-American President through two terms, and she'll probably live through the next president's consecutive terms in office. She raised 3 children... alone. Tears fall as I write, the thought of having to raise my 3 children without their dad is saddening, I'm blessed to have him. My father was her only son. Jerome passed away the day before his first born granddaughters', 1st birthday. His spirit is still strongly present among us. He never knew his father. It's not the typical story of an absent dad; he was killed, prior to my dad's birth. Daddy spoke of him as if he knew him, stories he heard pictures he saw... but my father was proud of his father. The absence did infect his life and my dad's departure infiltrates ours. My grandmother has never spoken of it. As a little girl I wondered why? Why no stories or memories told of Grandfather Charles? I wanted to know more about him, was he as strong as people said he was? Did my dad look like him, why was my dad's nickname Punkin? A grown woman, now I comprehend why she didn't discuss the pass. Loss is painful, and she's experienced it abundantly.

My maternal Grandmother, Thelma had 7 children. I admired her. The love I felt for her then, survives today. It has everything to do with my mom's loving way and gifted ability to soothe others. I have great childhood memories at Grandma's house. I played with cousins, dogs, on tire swings, biked and helped with the pigs and attending the garden with Grandpa Fred. I remember family cookouts, holidays and sitting on the porch while the dogwoods were in full bloom, and scents of roses and peonies filled my nose. My babysitter; she shared duties with my mom. She even pressed my hair with a hot comb. Like my hair, I thrived – evidence of meticulous care. I can't recall when she became blind. Challenged with Diabetes and Leukemia, she was

Challenge into Change

my hero. I wasn't omniscient, I never heard talk of defeat, or despair. I didn't know what she was going through. There wasn't a pity party. One day, I sat back against her bathroom door crying. She was sick-vomiting; I didn't want her to die. When she opened the bathroom door distraught, she assured me, loved me, and I was relieved. All would be fine. She always made me feel I was special and precious.

I often ask, "How did they do it?" A voice answers, "With God all things are possible." With the faith I inherited, I gained strength, courage, hope, love, and character. A priceless heirloom, to pass on to my three daughters, Inscribed, "One strong woman begets an-other."

How our judges and readers responded...

This is an expansive story of grandmotherly care, lost memories, and family tradition. ♥ *By threading together accounts of four generations, you communicate both the stories you have inherited and the legacy you entrust to your daughters.*

BIO:

I'm Monique- a wife, mother of three, a sister, and a daughter. I believe in equal rights and justice. I'm an advocate for young girls and women. During the day, I work for a non-profit org. specializing in environmental protections in Accounts Payable. I have an entrepreneurial spirit! My interests are broad, and varied. My family is my first priority. I'm a native of Orange County, VA I attended ODU, and worked for UVA 9+ yrs.

Challenge into Change

My Promise
Janet Centini

There simply wasn't enough space in my son's small bedroom for all of us. I looked around and did the only thing that seemed logical at the moment: I asked my husband to help me climb into my son's hospital bed. That allowed his sister, brother, dog and his dad to gather a bit closer. On the periphery, our family doctor, my parents and the parish priest knelt and prayed. The hospice nurse sat just outside the door. I let Jeff's head rest on my shoulder and I whispered to him "we'll be okay. I promise you. And you will be too. More than okay. I promise." As the sun filtered through the newly budded spring green leaves, I repeated the words of promise over and over I don't know how many times. I only knew one thing: I had given birth to Jeff over 16 years earlier and I wasn't going to let him die without me by his side. With each labored breath, I was filled with something that will forever stay with me: an unconditional love and a clarity unlike anything I had ever experienced. As he took his last breath, the room filled with cries. I felt a soft breeze from the open window on my tear-streaked face and was overwhelmed by such a grace-filled gratitude even as my heart was breaking.

As the next days, weeks and months melted into one another, I watched as our family began the process of living without one of us. I remember the first time my youngest son took out plates to set the table for dinner: five place settings. Then as he placed them around the table, he broke into tears as he remembered we only needed four now. I marveled at how my daughter finished her first year at college while grieving so for her brother and the love they shared. I ached as my husband built a stonewall with tons of different size rocks because he needed to do something with his grief. What did I do? I kept my promise to my son.

Challenge into Change

For the past 12 years, I learned so much about myself. I am not the same person I was before his cancer diagnosis. His death has taught me the life is quite precious and filled with startling paradox. I have learned that a broken heart has more space for compassion, that tears can make a garden grow, that even after the darkest day magnificent sunshine is possible and that the cries of those who suffer can learn to laugh again. I understand the saying Love Never Dies as I love Jeff more today than I did 12 years ago. Most importantly, I have kept the promise I made to him: we are okay and I believe, more than anything, that he is too.

How our judges and readers responded...

Heartbreaking—after loss of child, this mother learns to carry on for herself and her family. ♥ *This author's story moved me to tears. She wrote it so well you could feel her grief, the grief of a mother who's dealt with the unthinkable- the death of a child. What's even more remarkable is where she is 12 years later, having kept that promise to her son.* ♥ *The quiet beauty of this piece is in its cadence and rhythm that take the reader through a slow dance of tragedy to blossom into something redeeming and graceful.* ♥ *Well done. Very impressive and really rivets the reader. Keep writing.*

BIO:

After years as a stay at home mom, I started my own part-time business as a college admissions advisor to high school students and their families. I assist in all aspects of the college admission process. I also volunteer for Hospice of the Piedmont in bereavement support groups. For the past 9 years, I have held various positions on the UVA Children's Hospital Committee, most recently as the Committee Chair. I returned to school after my son's death in 2004 and graduated with honors from UVA - a lifelong dream. I am the mother of three, have a yellow lab named Jake, a grandpuppy and an extremely supportive husband. I enjoy reading, travel, hiking and an occasional glass of Chardonnay!

No Hay Tiempo Para Llorar
Lilian Cerna

Traer a mi mente recuerdos malos y buenos no es fácil para resumir mi vida, donde hay malos recuerdos que abundan. Vengo de una familia disfuncional, un padre maltratador y una madre sumisa. Cuando uno es pequeño, los maltratos físicos, verbales, abuso de alcohol, ver acompañantes inadecuados, uno piensa que todo es normal porque vive inmerso en ese mundo y se acostumbra a eso. Vi muchas veces golpeada a mi madre hasta el punto de verla casi muerta. Esas imágenes no se borran, los sonidos no se olvidan, pero ella siempre estuvo ahí porque era amor.

A través de los años la vida me enseñó a pasar cosas muy duras, desde enfrentamientos con mi padre, bajezas y llegar a pasar necesidades económicas, hasta no tener un techo ni alimento. Pero nunca había tiempo para lamentarse ni nadie que se preocupara de cómo me sentía.

Así pasé 10 años de mi vida, incluyendo la adolescencia donde necesitas guías y apoyo y no lo hubo; tuve muchas libertades no hubo límites porque nadie estuvo ahí. Mi padre en su mundo, con su nueva mujer joven, con otros hijos; y mi madre llorando para que el regrese y a la vez buscando afecto en otros hombres.

En esta etapa vi muchos caer en drogas y malas compañías, pero eso no quise para mí y me alejé de todo e ingresé a la Universidad y a trabajar. Era una vida con muchas responsabilidades, pero igual independiente ya que en casa no cambiaba nada solo los roles.

Llega la etapa de conocer a tu pareja y piensas que todo lo que viste no debe pasar, pero me toco un hombre irresponsable y mantenido por lo que tuve que dejar a mi hija con mi familia para que ella no vea separaciones, sufrimiento, ni pase necesidades. Pasó un largo tiempo para poder tenerla.

Challenge into Change

Cuando llega a mí, pasamos uno de los peores momentos de vida: la lucha legal contra un abusador sexual y ver como las amistades y familia no te apoyan porque el abusador era conocido y a nadie le importa el hecho; ni la pareja que tenía en esos momentos que también quería maltratarme y no me deje y por eso nos separamos de inmediato.

En esta vida pase muchas veces sin saber el significado de una navidad por estar sola o, aunque estaba con mis padres, igual era frio ver la desvalorización de una persona que no importa que los hijos sean lastimados que no le importara nada. Muchas veces hundirme en alcohol hasta casi ver la muerte dije "estoy tocando fondo" pero así salí sola.

Actualmente soy profesional, tengo 2 carreras y me he dedicado mucho a instruirme, en auto educarme y llegar a obtener cargos muy importantes con bastante responsabilidad.

Tengo una familia constituida, estoy casada, tenemos un hijo que amo mucho, esta una hijastra que también comparto con ella. Pero la vida no es completa porque tenía a mi hija a mi lado, pero para que no caiga en las cosas feas de esta juventud tuvo que irse con mi familia y no es fácil para mí.

Por todo esto que pase y estoy pasando no he tenido tiempo para llorar, solo pensar cómo salir de esto también…

Cómo respondieron nuestros jueces y lectores...

¡De la adversidad al éxito! Tu historia es una muestra perfecta de que es posible vencer las adversidades que se nos presentan en la vida y alcanzar el éxito.. ♥ Gracias por compartir esos recuerdos de tu infancia y por recordarnos que si se puede salir adelante. ♥ Tu valentía y perseverancia son lecciones de vida para todo el que lee tu historia. ♥ Nos hablas de un comienzo muy angustiante en el viaje de tu vida. Y, sin embargo, este viaje ha tenido un final triunfal. Es obvio que tienes muchos recursos internos.

Biografía:

Mi nombre es Lilian Cerna Cartes de nacionalidad Chilena, residi en Ecuador alrededor de 38 anos donde realice todos mis estudios. Soy Psicologa Clinica y Educadora Especial. Trabaje por 11 anos en inclusion educativa y discapacidad la cual obtuve un reconocimiento en el periodico por dicha labor, represente a Ecuador como panelista en el Congreso internacional de discapacidad. Como Psicologa Clinica tengo distintos cursos, talleres y congresos asistidos, mi labor ha sido en diversas areas desde trabajo en drogodependencia, personas con VIH, violencia intrafamiliar y consulta privada con ninos, adolescentes y adultos. Trabaje por 4 anos para el Gobierno del Ecuador para Red INFA en el rescate de ninos, ninas y adolescentes maltratados y abusados sexualmente,dictar talleres sobre el maltrato infantil, talleres de convivencia familiar y escolar y sobre violacion sexual: Ministerio de Salud Publica, asistiendo a pacientes, dictando talleres de diferentes enfermedades infectocontagiosas, ETS y mas: y el Ministerio de Justicia, Derechos Humanos y Cultos llegando a ser Directora de Evaluacion y Diagnostico de personas privadas de libertad en la carcel de varones de Guayaquil. Actualmente resido en Estados Unidos con mi esposo e hijos y estoy cursando una Maestria en psicologia infantil.

There's No Time for Tears
(English translation from Spanish)
Lilian Cerna

Bringing back good and bad memories does not come easy to me, especially while summarizing my life where the bad memories abound. I come from a dysfunctional family, an abusive father and a submissive mother. When one is small, the physical and verbal battering, alcohol abuse, and being surrounded by the wrong kind of people, could be perceived as normal because we live immersed in that world and we are used to it. I often saw my mom being beaten until the point of seeing her almost dead. Those images and sounds are not easy to forget, but she stayed there because she thought it was love.

Throughout the years life has taught me to confront very difficult situations, from confrontations with my father, poverty, not having a roof over my head or food on the table. However, there was no time to lament as there was no one who would worry about me.

This is how I lived for over 10 years of my life, even through adolescence which is a period when you need guidance and support, but there wasn't any. I had all the freedom in the world as there were no limits for me because nobody was there. My father lived in his own world with his new young woman and his new family; and my mother crying for his return and looking for affection in other men at the same time.

During this time, I saw many people fall into drugs and bad company, but I did not want that for me and I left, got accepted at a University and started to work. It was a life with many responsibilities, but I was still independent because at home nothing changed only the roles.

Later on I met who I thought would be my partner and I thought that everything I had lived and experienced should not happen to me, unfortunately I met a very irresponsible and lazy man and I was forced to leave my daughter with my family as I did not want her to suffer through a separation. A long time had to pass until I got her back.

When I finally got her back, we experienced the worst moments of our lives. I faced a legal feud against a sexual abuser and I got to see how friends and family refused to show me any kind of support because the abuser was a well know person among our circle of friends and family. I could tell that no one cared, not even my partner who tried to mistreat me so I decided to leave him immediately.

I have spent most of this life not knowing the true meaning of Christmas, due to the fact that I was always alone, even when I was with my parents I felt alone; it was demoralizing seeing how someone could not care less that their children are hurt. There were plenty of times that I almost drank myself to death until I finally hit rock bottom and decided to get back on my feet, all on my own.

Nowadays I am a professional and I managed to obtained two degrees. I have dedicated my time to teaching myself and being responsible to the point where I now have very important positions at my job.

I have formed a well-structured and stable family, I am married now and I have a son who I love very much as well as a step-daughter, however I still feel that my life is not complete as my daughter still lives with my family which is not easy for me.

Due to everything I went through and still am going through I feel there is no time for tears, only time to think how to once again overcome this…

Challenge into Change

How our judges and readers responded...

Challenge into change! Your story is a perfect example that it is possible to overcome adversity and achieve success. ♥ Thank you for sharing those childhood memories and for reminding us that we can change our lives for the better. ♥ Your courage and perseverance are life lessons for everyone who reads your story. ♥ You tell us about a very harrowing beginning to your life's journey. And yet this journey has had a triumphant ending. You must have so many inner resources.

BIO:

My name is Lilian Cerna Cartes, of Chilean nationality. I lived in Ecuador for 38 years where I completed all my studies. I am a clinical psychologist and special educator. I worked for 11 years in educational inclusion and disability, for which work I obtained recognition in the newspaper, and represented Ecuador as a panelist at the International Disability Congress. As a clinical psychologist I have different courses, workshops and assisted conferences, my work has been in various areas from work in drug addiction, people with HIV, domestic violence and private consultation with children, adolescents and adults. I worked for 4 years for the Government of Ecuador for INFA Network in the rescue of mistreated and sexually abused children and adolescents, gave workshops on child abuse, workshops on family and school life and sexual abuse; Ministry of Public Health, assisting patients, providing workshops on different infectious diseases, STDs, and more; and, the Ministry of Justice, Human Rights and Worship where I became the Director of Evaluation and Diagnosis for persons deprived of liberty in Men's Prison of Guayaquil. I am currently residing in the United States with my husband and children and I am pursuing a master's degree in child psychology.

The Journey of Life
Eleanor L. Crichlow

Life is a small word, but it is the beginning of your journey on earth from the time you take your first breath and the challenges you have to try and overcome. At the age of seventy-three I look back at the many I have had to come to terms with and in my own way emotionally deal with, some were greater than others, but each one at different times affected me as a young child, a woman, wife and mother.

I was raised in a lower to middle class family of hard workers, but alcohol, fighting and sexual abuse had its place behind closed doors. The hidden don't tell secrets as you grow up thinking this is all normal and not aware that it destroys confidence and self-esteems. Until you realize emotionally you are a disaster in a pressure cooker waiting to explode.

It took years of walking down the wrong path in life. I did not pull great grades in school, I was lucky enough to graduate out of high school my parents were not as lucky they both had to leave school to go to work. It was not so unusual in those days in large families. My parents, aunts and uncles drank and partied not to feel the pain of life the way it worked out for them. Unfortunately, the children of the family and not just my immediate family, but my cousins as well felt it changed the courses of our lives, when we spoke about it in later years.

At the age of nineteen I married my first husband and at this time in my life I realized that I was in no way prepared for marriage or to have children and because of it the marriage lasted just about eight years. My husband married shortly after the marriage broke up. Picking up the pieces were not easy but I managed to put myself through cosmetology school so I could support my children and living with my parents also needed financial help. I did get a great hairdressing

Challenge into Change

79

position at an up scaled salon and worked there for several years and met my second husband.

I had six children and he had two they ranged in age from sixteen down to six all lived under our roof. This was truly a challenge in so many ways for both of us. My husband and his children came from living in the South and me and mine born and raised in the North. Cultural differences were apparent.

My husband and I endured the pressures for thirty years of our marriage and the extended problems with children. We are now separated almost ten years. We still keep as a family; it was not a question about love, that still exists. It was losing each other in process.

Blessed as woman for the challenges I have overcome, and working today as a secretary in my parish. I feel that I was never alone on the journey of life.

How our judges and readers responded...

This is a great story. You pay attention to both the grandiose and minute details of your journey called life. I really enjoyed reading it. ♥ *You express the hardships you and your family experienced so clearly and straightforwardly — but these descriptions are perhaps all the more moving for that.* ♥ *Thank you for sharing this intensely personal and yet powerful, inspiring story.*

Got Lemons? Make Lemonade!
Jill Watson Clark

Santa is making a list and checking it twice;

it's a time of year he reviews everyone's life and Christmases past.

My list would be an interesting, happy, sad, and everything in-between kind of list:

- Birth of babies x 2 and grandkids x 4
- Marriages x 2
- Career highs and lows
- Illnesses
- Raped at age 21
- Being divorced and now a widow
- Death of parents

Twin brother to suicide

Husband

Family members

Friends

And the list goes on…

So, someone who struggled being a single mom for 11+ years,

someone who questioned why her brother no longer could choose to live,

someone who has worked their entire life, and

someone who was obese and dealt with the health issues that accompany obesity,

it would have been very easy to have pity parties and have a "Whoa is me attitude."

I chose, instead, to be grateful for my many blessings and not to dwell on all that's not good. It's the is the glass half empty or half full? I lie in bed in the wee early hours of a new day and say "Today's going to be a good day."

It's irrelevant that the weather forecast is for snow and ice or for 100 plus degrees.

You have a plan A; when you realize that's just no longer an option

then you go on to plan B or to plan C.

You also remind yourself of the Serenity Prayer and if totally realizing you cannot,

under any circumstances change or alter something,

then move on to other, more important things that you can influence.

One of my prouder moments was the fact that just prior to my 60th Birthday,

I realized I had no one to take care of me.

If I couldn't do that, then my health was going to continue to spiral out of control and I couldn't save the world if I couldn't myself!

I lost 96 pounds and went on a zip line!

It's important for all women, regardless of the obstacles in this thing we call life,

take responsibility, do what we think is right at the time,

and surround ourselves with family and friends who support and encourage us.

Twenty plus years every Thursday, the Thursday Lunch Bunch gathers to do just that.

How blessed I am. And I thank the Lord for the good and the not so good. It has shaped me into who I am today.

I've won awards for my work mentoring children. I was named Waynesboro's Outstanding Women in 2013 for volunteerism. Now don't get me wrong. Awards are nice, but what is far more important is at the end of the day when I lay my head down on my pillow, I can say to myself

"Well done"...

How our judges and readers responded...

What a moving poem of optimism and gratitude. ♥ *You make really good use of the simplicity of the list form to aptly convey how the difficulties you've faced have not made you listless or cynical.* ♥ *Your story is a testament of just how much women are capable of in spite of – or because of – the challenges they face.* ♥ *Thank you for sharing it.*

BIO:

I am retired from DeJarnette Center, a children's psychiatric hospital. I currently mentor young children. I married twice and am currently a widow. I am a Nana to so many. My volunteering includes: serving as Chairperson, Waynesboro Electoral Board; hosting Waynesboro Generals baseball coaches and players for the summer baseball season. I love the Lord and serve on many mission trips. I love to travel, camp, scrapbook, spending time with family and friends, and eating!

Challenge into Change

She Is Me
Carnegie Clatterbaugh

She's fun,
but she's not together.

She's cute,
but she's not together.

She's disarray,
hair in a clip,
purse a mess.
she's not together.

Tattered magazine,
late again.

Time is irrelevant,
she's not together.

She's there,
but not all there.

She's never home,
but thinks she's alone.

She's not together,
but I love her anyway..................

How our judges and readers responded…

I absolutely love this piece. ♥ *The repetition is stunning and somehow draws me closer to the "She". I feel close to her. I relate to not being "together," to being in "disarray," and "a mess".* ♥ *The title of the piece tells us that the author also relates to the "She" but the use of third person makes me think that the author does not wish to identify with "She" completely. Nevertheless, at the end of the poem "She" receives love from the author, bringing the poem to an emotionally moving conclusion.*

The Lost Child

Brianna Cousins

All I ever wanted was the perfect family. Me? I didn't. I had a dysfunctional family. Some may ask what a dysfunctional family is. A dysfunctional family is a family in which conflict, misbehavior, and often child neglect or abuses on the part of individual parents occur continually and regularly, leading other members to accommodate such actions. There are different roles a child plays being a part of a dysfunctional family. I would identify my role as the "lost child". Most times I felt fortunate to live with both parents and my older sibling. But sometimes I felt my family was different from others around me. Growing up my father was the stern, supportive, church-going parent. My mother was the works all night- sleep all day, emotionally detached parent. My brother was the "problem child." Living in a household with different personalities and a lack of communication between each of us was difficult. As a child you want to spend quality time, feel loved and supported by both parents. That is where my anger and frustration came from because I didn't get the attention, approval or support I searched for. That led me to becoming the "lost child " trying to escape family situations by making myself withdraw from reality.

Throughout my adolescent years I faced much pain from being bullied, misused, touched inappropriately, and being peer pressured. I wanted to tell my parents but felt too embarrassed because there was no true connection where I comfortably felt opened to telling my parents anything. My parents were to busy with their own lives that made me think I was invisible and unheard. I wasn't the only one though in the household that felt that way because my brother made it loud and clear that he wasn't receiving the proper attention. So he turned to the streets seeking a love that he couldn't find which ended him in and out of juvenile several times and with a six year sentence by the time he was 21 years old. To witness firsthand your sibling being taken away by the authorities is heartbreaking but to know that you will have to live without them for awhile is even more heartbreaking. Suddenly my family started became very bitter and I became even more distant.

As I got into my adult years I noticed that certain behaviors worsened such as forming wrong relationships, being promiscuous, experimenting with drugs and alcohol, and suffering from an abortion. For years I intentionally wanted to avoid attention and fade into the background, retreating into my own world. I was able to function in my own world with much emotional chaos around me, and be truly unaffected by intense emotions because it was what I was most comfortable with.

I was truly the "lost child" and didn't think it was possible of changing. I remember when I was 21 it was a New Year's Eve night when I decided to visit a local church. Prior to that night I had plans on going to the club but the Lord led me to church. That service was an unforgettable experience which led me to eventually join the church. In one particular service the pastor prayed for me and I immediately felt a shift happening as he prophesied over my life. I became more God-focused instead of people focused. The Holy spirit had showed me to forgive and let go, and pray for my family. I was obedient to his direction and he opened my eyes to love my family despite of hurt, rejection, and past experiences. Here it is 4 years later and I am now 25 with my own family that God has blessed me with. Even though the enemy will try to come into my thoughts and try to discourage me from being the parent God wants me to be I immediately block it and speak against it. I am now able to love freely with God's help and he's able to use my weakness for his glory. I hope this inspires each parent to be the best they can be to their child.

Challenge into Change

How our judges and readers responded…

Your description of your family is strong and vivid, and made me feel your sense of isolation as a child. ♥ *The way that your story comes full circle, to your own children, makes it a powerful one.* ♥ *Your faith has given you the strength to live as you wish to.* ♥ *You story will surely inspire others.*

BIO:

Hello. My name is Brianna Cousins and I'm from Richmond Va. I'm 25 years young with a beautiful family. I have worked in many different work fields but feel most called to empowering and uplifting women of all ages. I'm not a writer but I chose to be bold and take advantage of this wonderful opportunity to tell my story and hopefully it can inspire many.

Taking the Scenic Route
Stephanie Rose DeNicola

In the fall of 1999 I was a strong, confident & healthy 22-year-old woman. It was supposed to be my last semester in college in Pennsylvania before student teaching. I had spent 6 years focused on becoming a high school English teacher and I could see the end coming. Six weeks into the semester I woke up and lost the use of the left side of my body. I was rushed to the ER. Doctors thought it was a stroke or brain tumor. I was unable to walk, write my name, feed myself or use the bathroom alone. It took 13 doctors six weeks to diagnose me with extremely severe rheumatoid arthritis -- at 22. Standard treatment is chemotherapy every week for the rest of your life. I was told teaching in a conventional classroom could kill me. I packed up my things and moved back home to Queens. Six months later I found a medication cocktail that worked – an infusion every 6 weeks which I have been taking for 16 years now which makes me the longest running person on the drug. I became a pharmacy tech and learned how medications worked. I took a job in DC a year, learned to drive then moved west to Virginia over several years. In 2005 I took a job as an environmental educator. They wanted someone who liked teaching – I wanted health insurance. I had a steep learning curve but nearly 12 years later I am the top environmental educator in VA and advise on regional and statewide policy. I'm married, have a 5-year-old daughter and I finished the 2001 Honolulu Marathon (10 hours 56 minutes) and the 2002 Bermuda Half-Marathon (5 hours 6 minutes). I joke that I took the scenic route to teaching – and every day is a gift. I also get where I'm going – I'm just a little slower than I used to be!

Challenge into Change

How our judges and readers responded…

This story exudes positivity. ♥ *By describing your recovery as "the scenic route," you emphasize the flexibility and resilience that helped you, at long last, become a teacher.*

BIO:

Stephanie earned a B.A. in English from Mansfield University of Pennsylvania. Stephanie completed a year of national service as an AmeriCorps Promise Fellow in DC. She helps newly diagnosed arthritis patients cope with their illness and teaches them how to become their own healthcare advocate. She also volunteers as a patient success story for Johnson and Johnson and is featured in the "Patient Perspective" program of the American College of Rheumatology. Stephanie lives with her husband and daughter.

Against All Odds
Marian Dixon

Against all odds is all I can say of this dear lady's work and heart. She walks in faith in spite of all blocks and trials formed along the way.

The first African American in many a field; a license nurse, computer programmer, counselor, Apostle, teacher, preacher with many degrees in bible studies and a singer.

She pastors two churches, prison, jail Ministry, feeds the homeless, has a thrift store and many other things she does.

Against all odds she works to win people back to God, for freedom, health, peace and out of control of sins.

She is a medical miracle in the medical took due to an operation for cancer, unexplained lumps were removed from her body, the doctor said would cause paralysis if removed.

The doctor removed cancer from her throat, said when removed she would need a voice box after to talk, preach or sing. She woke up speaking after surgery and now preaches, teaches, and sings louder than before.

What a jewel of a person – who stands against all odds. Strong in faith and believe what God say – not man, loves people from her heart, helps anyone she can,

What a jewel of a person – who stands against all odds – against all odds.

Challenge into Change

How our judges and readers responded…

"It's truly a blessing to have someone in our lives who helps us be strong simply by being strong themselves. ♥ Your writing is lyrical in its refrain of "against all odds," naming the many ways this woman gives of herself, serves others, breaks down barriers, even as she conquered cancer. ♥ You clearly treasure this "jewel of a person." I would love to meet this "jewel of a person." She has been heroic in so many ways!"

The Angel
Mary Dudley Eggleston

I was dressed in Wellington boots and Levi jeans, naked from the waist up and in a room with two strange men—both dressed from the waist up in white coats, neckties, and stethoscopes. Something didn't feel right. I asked the student doctor if I was his first. He said no, but examined my breast like a ninth grader. I tried to focus on the pewter angel that lived in my pocket. I carried it with me everywhere, in case I found myself in a bad spot—like being half-naked at age forty-nine with a surgeon and his third-year med student, about to have a cancerous blob cut out of my right breast.

My heart raced in outpatient surgery. Running away made more sense than waiting for my turn with the surgeon. I gave my angel another cold, clammy squeeze, desperate to believe everything would be alright. But my gut kept rolling.

I told the anesthesiologist that I wanted to be awake; that I wanted to know what was going on. He said okay, but that he would monitor me closely and put me under if he thought I needed it. I told him that I wanted to keep my pewter angel with me. He wrapped it in surgical tape to insulate it against sparks and fire and damnation and reluctantly let me hold it in the palm of my hand. I breathed deeply for the first time that day.

A nurse helped me onto the operating table and put a seatbelt around my legs. I wondered if I was going somewhere. He pulled my arms out perpendicular, laid them on table extensions and threaded them through cotton sheaths. Everything about me was tied down. Someone covered my hands with blue paper sheets and then covered all of me—even my face. Only the right half of my chest was exposed. Did they not want me to see them? Or did they not want to see me? As the third of four daughters, I have been invisible most of my life. I wanted them to see me, so I wiggled my right hand free from the paper sheet and stretched it open. Someone covered it back up.

Challenge into Change

In my post-op-truth-serum-state-of-mind I told the med student to think of his patient as if it's her first time and to treat her as if she's his daughter or his mother, so he would truly see her. Without thinking, I gave him my angel. He paused and raised his surgeon's mask. As he unwrapped the surgical tape, he told me his name and that he was from the flatlands of Nebraska. I told him mine, and that I was from the mountains of Virginia. He said he had two daughters, twelve and eleven. I said I had two sons, sixteen and fourteen, and smiled as our eyes met.

How our judges and readers responded...

The way in which the story summons your own personal totem, your angel, is quite moving. ♥ *Your descriptions of the hospital environment are arresting, as are the moments of real connection between doctors and patient.* ♥ *How fortunate you were to meet a compassionate doctor at this time in your life.* ♥ *Yes, it is so important to be seen and understood.*

BIO:

Mary Dudley Eggleston is retired and lives in Nelson County.

My Tutor and My Friend
Sharon W. Eldridge

The one person I admire is my tutor Judy White. First of all Judy is a really nice person and easy to talk to about anything. Second she also is a retired schoolteacher and she volunteers at the UVA hospital. Finally I admire Judy because she is so giving of herself, and she didn't stop teaching but most of all she believes me.

First of all Judy is a really nice caring person, and easy to talk to about anything. She's our tutor she has been for years now, she's not just our tutor that we see on Mondays, Wednesdays of every week. She's a friend, I come to class straight from work and sometimes she can just look at me, and can tell what kind of day I have had and she cares about that so she listens. Then she asks me how can we use that life experience Sharon? And write about it, she makes you think, you use everything we give her as a teaching opportunity and I admire this skill in you Judy.

She's not only my tutor two days out of a week, she's a retired schoolteacher, and she volunteers at the UVA hospital. This is another reason why I admire Judy she's retired and she's still on the move taking care of others only that she's a wife, mother, grandmother, not once have I heard her complain. She also finds time to take care of herself by walking and drinking plenty of water. Judy also travels with her husband Bill. When I look at Judy I can see that she really loves and enjoy her life and takes nothing for grant and I admire this in her.

Here's another reason why I admire Judy because she is so giving of herself, and she didn't stop teaching but most of all she believes in me. When a person pours so much of themselves into you all you want to do is make them proud. She this kind of person, I remember when I told her that I can't think of anything to write about. She didn't want to hear that, she would say come on Sharon; you have a

Challenge into Change

lot to say. It's funny now, because now I ask her to give me something to write about now. This is what I'm talking about when I say about she pours herself into you which makes you want to try harder to get to the next level. I can tell that she is and was a good teacher because once it's in you to help others succeed she will help you, as long as you put forth the effort to help yourself as well. She believes in me this is why she pushes me so hard to believe in myself.

Finally I haven't run across to many people that I can say that I truly admire. Judy Thank you for being so caring, nice, and taking time out of your busy life to inspire, and tutor me. You have shown me that you are never too old to learn if there's one like you willing to teach you, and you have taught me to never give up on a dream. And you have also taught me that giving of your time to help people is very important and satisfying. As you can see Judy White is the one person I admire.

How our judges and readers responded…

What a lovely tribute! ♥ *I am sure that this essay will make Judy very happy* ♥ *After reading this, I can picture Judy in my head thanks to your exacting attention to detail.*

BIO:

My name is Sharon Washington Eldridge. I am a native of Charlottesville. I currently work at UVA and have been there for 20 years. At this time, I am nearing completion of the National External Diploma Program. I will earn my high school diploma from Charlottesville City Schools in early 2017. I am married with two daughters and two grandsons.

For Steve, but Really for Me
Elizabeth

I have been known
To misconstrue sex and love.
Two sides of the milky way.
From a distance there are resemblances,
A parallel universe, the same.
Yet up close
And personal
They are worlds apart, like galaxies
Strewn among the stars
Wrenched apart
A great divide
In all their physicality
Sharing no resemblance,
just seemingly so, but fraught with angst
A whisper of a wish
Once uttered and surrendered, this.

Where Hermes and Aphrodite flee
Beyond the stars
In ages past
A myth beyond our time, yet now resounding
Not a whisper but a shout for future reckoning
And love. To Lesbos in a time of wild, wild seas
And free, but now distressed each refugee
To be, to love
No sense of Ovid's past or
Sappho's sands so black at sea
But just
To be, to love, true love.

A voice, as Sirens cry
Or rather, scream aloud
Both shy and proud

Challenge into Change

Smashing against the rocks, so loud
A voice is found! A choice both inside,
And outside beyond the noise.
And reckoning begins amidst the seas
With shifting winds continuing to blow.
A firm resolve to trust and know
Oneself
And share that love within, without
And hope that it resounds about.
But mostly just to learn to love the one,
Not Zeus, the greatest of them all,
But simply, though no longer small,
Of greater stature than appears
The witness, bearing all
Standing here - And standing tall.

How our judges and readers responded…

Exploring the way that sex and love might look the same but are wildly different makes a strong subject for a poem. ♥ *I love that the poem is deeply personal but also universal, and that you make its universal claims clear with references to classical myth.* ♥ *Great title! You use classical allusions so well. The love one has for oneself is the source of all love. That is an idea to ponder.*

BIO:

The Women's Initiative has given me the courage to write, to process, and to share.

My Mother's News
Dabney Farmer

This past month, I noticed Mom was more tired than usual.
Sleep keeps overcoming her.

She sees the doctor, but doesn't get her results back that day...
Or the next day,
Or even the day after that.

Saturday, she gets a call from the doctor.
Doctors never call on Saturdays...
Unless...

They tell her they need to have another test.
Another test? That's not good.
Think positive.
Still no results on the following day.
No results the next day either
Or the day after that.
Another day. Still, no results.
Then one night at dinner my mother says, "I got my results."
So many days had passed that I had almost forgotten...
Almost, being the key word.
I'm hoping she will say, "I'm alright.
But she didn't.
Instead, she says "I have a brain tumor,"

At that moment I felt like I was hit by a train.
A tumor the size of my thumb is in my mother's brain.

The doctors say it been there for more than ten years.

Mom assures me it's not cancer,
The tumor is benign.
But still, it's still a bloody tumor.

A month after Mom's surgery my Dad tells me Mom's still tired.
The doctors said that's normal.

Challenge into Change

After all, they dug a chunk of her head.
I don't correct him, and say it was her brain, not her head they cut.

Neither sounds pleasant.
And I know he doesn't like to think about her brain.
When the doctors showed Dad a photo of the removed tumor, he fainted.

The week is long and endless waiting for the final results that will change our family forever.
The once that say if the tumor is coming back or not.
Even worse than before, which I didn't think was even possible.

Every day I go to sleep worrying myself sick.
Will tomorrow be the worst day of my life?
Or the best when Mom gets a clean bill of health.

Then, one day my mom comes home and says...
"Oh yeah, I got the results back today, I'm fine."
The weight of the world lifts off my shoulders.

That is until my mom adds...
"They want to see me again in six months."

"SIX! You said they only want to see you once a year!"
"They said six." Now Let's get dinner ready, will you help?" my Mom asks.
Of course I help. What daughter wouldn't help at this moment?

Mom gives me a big hug.
"I'm not going anywhere," she says.
"I know," I say out loud hugging her back tight.
But in my mind I say. "For how long?"

How our judges and readers responded...

The staccato tone of these lines and the sudden perfect rhymes capture the pain and subtle absurdity of tending to a sick loved one. ♥ *The way the piece moves pushes the reader along just as one might interact with an overwhelming hospital system. It has an incredibly levity about it while delivering a story of great weight and import.* ♥ *Very moving.* ♥ *You describe the emotions associated with a dreaded diagnosis so well. I hope your mother stays healthy!*

BIO:

Dabney Farmer lives with her family in Charlottesville Virginia.

From Couch Surfing to Skydiving – A Tale of Surviving Domestic Violence
B. Faulkner

It was my birthday. Thirty-five years old, and my boyfriend texted, telling me not to come home, that we were done. Then I had to administer state exams. I cried silently while monitoring the students. Somehow, I survived the day, and picked my daughter up from school. He gave me that evening to get my belongings out of our home where I thought we were building something and would live together forever. He was moving another girl in, and, coincidentally, it was her birthday, too.

I packed what would fit in my car, paring our lives down to the essentials—her medical equipment, enough clothes for a while, toiletries, mementos, my fairy wings. A lady never leaves home without her wings.

Nadia finished the last week of school and then went to her dad's for summer. I couch-surfed and began the long process of healing. I was mad at myself because I had let him beat me—stayed with him after he got black-out drunk, accused me of being a Russian spy, and shoved me, causing me to fall down in our kitchen, hit my head, and have a seizure. The mistake I made was believing his cries of, "Baby, I'm sorry. It won't happen again. Please forgive me. I'll get help."

And so I stayed, and the abuse became more frequent. Soon, he'd succeeded in isolating me from friends and family. Soon, his voice was all I could hear in my head, calling me fat, stupid, and worse. And somehow, although I've been independent since I was fifteen, won a full scholarship, earned a masters and an EdS, and became a National Board Certified teacher, I believed the nasty things he said to me, that I didn't deserve better, that the abuse WAS all my fault.

I stayed even after he started disappearing for days, leaving me to care for his young daughter, not calling. I later found out he was meeting women off Craigslist, doing drugs with them.

I spent that summer rediscovering self, visiting friends, camping, taking hours-long walks on the beach, kayaking, dancing frenetically at Phish shows. I vowed to never let someone take away my self-respect.

I discovered skydiving. I reclaimed my power by proving to myself that I wasn't stupid—I could learn to do something difficult, with little margin for error. I could think clearly and perform well under pressure. Perhaps because time stands still in those moments and nothing else matters except for what I am doing, jumping from planes has helped to soothe the traumatized parts of me.

I learned that I was in control, that every second counts and shouldn't be wasted joylessly. The only abusive relationship I am in now is with the ground. I don't have to lie about my bruises, bruises I earn when I have a rough encounter with the door of the plane on exit for example, or when I flare too early or too low.

I learned to let go. I learned to fly.

How our judges and readers responded…

This story juxtaposes two kinds of challenge, one that is agonizing and brutal and one that is exhilarating and empowering. ♥ *I love the moment when you pack up your fairy wings.* ♥ *Even as you describe one of your story's most painful moments, you hint at your transformation.*

BIO:

I am a high school English teacher, a mother, a poet, a skydiver, a scholar (trying to finish my dissertation). I want to teach other women to speak up for themselves, to not keep silent because of shame.

The Meaning of Her Rain
Veronica Haunani Fitzhugh

She lives in a pretty little box on a pretty little street. She has beautiful friends, a loving husband, and a sweet kitten named Bathsheba. She has it all.

She has depression.

She can't get out of her pretty little bed.

She decides she is the challenge she needs changing.

So, she learns about time travel, paper crafts, and child psychology and journeys back in time to teach her twelve year old self how to make the perfect umbrella for a rainy day.

She tries to lecture her former self about the meaning of the rain as she creates a clumsy origami crane. The crane's wingspan could not cover all of the little girl and eventually became a damp, pulpy mess that flew and fell away.

As the little, drenched girl begins to cry, her elder understands she must learn more about the rain's meaning before creating real shelter.

So, she revisits and studies every rainy day between her age of twelve to her new age of thirty eight with a camera.

She takes her years-worth of photos and binds them together with sturdy twine and her greatest expectations.

She sends the large photo journal through the time machine.

And, her new book of years of half, single, and double rainbows provides me cover in unexpected rain and hope of the coming sun.

Challenge into Change

How our judges and readers responded…

This poem uses inventive imagery to describe the process of self-discovery and healing. ♥ *The transition between the first stanza and the second stanza, when we learning that having "it all" includes having depression, jolts the reader's expectations.* ♥ *The representation of recovery as a kind of time travel is especially powerful.*

BIO:

Veronica Haunani Fitzhugh enjoys sipping Arnold Palmers while scribbling on her porch in Charlottesville, Virginia. She has a BA in English Literature from the University of Virginia. Her short works have been featured in several online and offline anthologies. She is currently working on something top secret and longer.

Desperation
Ebony Fletcher

After breaking up with my ex-boyfriend he came to my house two days later to kill me! On that day, I agreed to speak with. He was calm and sober. I repeated to him that we needed a break. At the time, I was working and going to school full time. We talked about getting back together and that conversation didn't go well at all. He pulled out a revolver out of his coat pocket and told me, "If I can't have you, nobody will!" My first thought was, I'm about to die at 24! I told him to calm down and go talk a walk. He tried to shoot me in my chest but I tried to get the gun out of his hand and he shot me in my right leg. We fought for the gun and I fell on the floor. He sat on my back so I couldn't move. He put the gun directly to my head and pulled the trigger but it jammed. He banged the gun against the wall several times and put it to my head again, it jammed. He banged it against the wall for a second time and it jammed. He did it again for the third time, put the gun to my head and pulled the trigger and IT WENT OFF! When you hear people say your life flashes before your eyes, right before your about to die, it's a true statement. Right before he pulled the trigger for the 3rd time, something said don't move, just lay there. I laid very still with my eyes closed and he got up and ran. I never seen him again after that. My journey after being shot wasn't easy. A lot of prayer and counseling. I wrote a very detailed 65-page business plan out of sheer anger and depression. I realized that I'm stronger than I thought I was and whatever life has to throw at me, I'm going to throw it right back. I'm here for a reason! I have invented 5 natural hair care product line that has reached 6 countries in the last 5 years and I'm so proud of myself. Everyone has a purpose in life..... a unique gift or special talent to give to others and the world. When we blend this unique talent with service to others, we experience the ecstasy and exultation of our own spirit, which is the ultimate goal of all goals!

Challenge into Change

How our judges and readers responded...

From the very first sentence, you tell a shocking story. ♥ *The details you include make your readers feel fear for your life then awe at your recovery.* ♥ *You've not only survived but flourished after your near-death experience.*

BIO:

Ms. Ebony Fletcher has 18 years' experience working in the cosmetology field. During her tenure as a cosmetologist, she has witnessed the changes and evolution of her industry and possesses the ideal background for managing and innovative business during the years of continued change to come. Ebony Fletcher graduated from Hair Design Institute in Bay Ridge, Brooklyn in 2006. She takes pride and excellence in helping people improve their appearance. She is a businessperson and has no doubt that her business venture will be a success. She created a natural hair care product in 2009 called, "Hair Krack" which curbs excessive hair loss.

My Past Life
Kamila FNU

The true story of my life. Now I'm 38 years old. I've seen a lot of challenges in my life. I was 17 years old, in my country there always was war. I have four brothers and four sisters. My second brother at 16 years old got lost. My village wasn't safe. My family decided to move because my father was a general.

Me and my two brothers lived with my big brother and his wife. They moved to Pakistan but my mom and father moved to the city. My life was very bad. I wasn't allowed to go to school because some people didn't allow their girls to go to school. I lived for 3 years with my brother in law. He always argued with the kids.

Then I went back to my country. There. I began to go to school. Then the Taliban came to Afghanistan and war started again. A rocket hit our house. I was with my father in the house, we were under the soil. They are the most horrible people in the world. The Taliban says all women couldn't go to school or have jobs. Women weren't allowed to leave the house. I stayed at home because the Taliban were very bad people.

One day, my sister and I went to shop. We went on the bus. A Taliban saw me and I didn't have my hijab on so he ran behind me. He stopped the bus, he came in the bus, and hit me with wires on my legs. He said "Why don't you have hijab?" I had no answer, only crying for me. My sister had her hijab on and she was also crying for me. She said "She will wear it next time." We both went back home. My legs had a lot of pain. I felt very scary and not well.

<u>My travel to Afghanistan</u>

On June 1st 2016, me and my children went to Afghanistan. My travel was too hard because with four children you have to keep up and take care of all 4 children. We stayed in Afghanistan 3 months. My two small girls everyday sick. I am busy with them and all my travel unhappy because my mom was very sick too. I spent three months with my family. Finally, it was over and we wanted to come back to the United States.

When we went to the airport, Afghanistan airport flight agent told me to give him my passport and when I gave him the passport, he checked up and told me "Your passport didn't pass." I was very sad. He gave me back our passports. We had to go back home. We had four suitcases and I was not able to carry them just by myself. It was hard.

I called my husband in the Unites States and asked him if he knew what happened and why was there a problem with our passports. He told me there wasn't any problem with the passports and not to worry, that everything will be ok. Because my English is not good, I mixed up the date of my flight and had to buy a more expensive ticket for another day. We stopped in the India Airport for five hours. Five terrible hours, I felt too terrible with the kids. The kids were sleeping in my arms. I was very tired. Later I started my other flight to New York airport. We stopped in New York for 4 hours. On the way to New York, my 4-year-old daughter was very sick. All the way she was crying in the airplane. I can't do it for her. My big problem was I didn't speak English for 3 months so I forgot my English, before my English was good.

Finally, we arrived to New York airport. Two bags on my shoulders and 2 kids holding my hands, and four suitcases. New York airport was new for me. I didn't know where to find my way to the place that gives out boarding passes. It was very hard to find the boarding passes.

My third flight was from New York to Washington D.C. When we arrived at the airport there were my husband and his friend waiting for us. He gave me a big hug and he gave the little ones a big hug too.

110   *Challenge into Change*

Then, we had to find our suitcases, one was broken and was wrapped in plastic. Then we all went home, we were very tired of the trip.

How our judges and readers responded...

I'm moved by this recollection of how your past and present lives converge at a moment when you went back to Afghanistan to visit your family. ♥ *It's so courageous of you to return after all that you've experienced there, and even more courageous of you to tell your story.* ♥ *I love that your story earnestly expresses tiredness and endurance, but also perhaps a glimmer of hope.*

BIO:

My English might be wrong – I'm sorry. My daughter Spozhmai helped me. She is in the 4th grade.

Challenge into Change

Learning to Like the Unlikeable
June Forte

Many of us run into someone we deeply dislike: a family member, a neighbor, a teacher. For me it was a coworker. He wasn't unpleasant. In fact he was quite friendly, but he would come into my office, sit by my desk, and proceed to discuss his daily work in great detail. He'd take an hour to explain a minor decision he made using a logic that I had never encountered and couldn't follow. He annoyed me. I had a full inbox to attend to myself, and I resented his constant intrusion. As time went by, my anger grew, and I was barely civil to him. Although he didn't seem to notice, I was avoiding eye contact with him as he droned on and on, and I realized my body language must be screaming for him to go away and leave me alone. Either he would notice or I would erupt in anger, and I really didn't want that to happen.

This was my problem and not his, so I looked for a way to change my attitude. I turned to the "Serenity Prayer," which is used in the Alcoholics Anonymous Program. Its core message is to accept what can't be changed, change what can, and be wise enough to know the difference. I accepted that I couldn't change this man, but I could change my reaction to him. I decided to challenge myself and find some reason to like him, one that would offset what I didn't like. And I did. I made the effort to observe and listened to him in the office and also in social settings.

What I discovered was that he was one of the most caring and generous people I have met. With that I was able to move away from the negative and zero in on the positive. We have both moved off into retirement, but we still call each other about twice a month to catch up. He still talks his decisions out ad nauseam, and it still annoys me, but having him as a friend far outweighs the annoyance. We now are old friends, and I wouldn't have it any other way.

How our judges and readers responded...

What a wonderful story—in the opening, I couldn't imagine what could be likable about this man, but by the end I had an image of someone who talks too much but has a kind heart. Your story inspires me to see good things in people that might initially seem nothing but irritating and impossible. ♥ *Your description of your anger at this man's intrusion is so vivid! I could feel my own body about to erupt in anger as I read it.* ♥ *You have written about an important life lesson. We are quick to judge (and reject) others when, in fact, we need to look again. Life can be so much richer when we look for the good in people.*

BIO:

June Forte is an award-winning journalist, photographer, editor and speechwriter. Her writing has appeared in the Washington Post, Chicago Tribune, the Colorado Springs Gazette-Telegraph, and in magazines as diverse as Woman's World, U.S. Medicine, Washington Golf Monthly and Aviation Digest. A career Civil Servant, she also taught communication courses at Northern Virginia Community College, in Woodbridge, Virginia, where she resides.

Challenge into Change

Una Familia que Emigra a USA

(Se cambiaron los nombres para proteger su privacidad)

Maria Godoy

En el 2005, Ruth emigró hacia los Estados Unidos en busca del sueño americano junto con su esposo Salomón y sus dos hijas: Milagro y Deborah. Al llegar, tuvo que enfrentar varios desafíos, desde los más básicos como el lugar donde vivirían, hasta cómo inscribir a sus hijas a la escuela, o cómo conseguir trabajo. Debió actuar con rapidez para resolver estos problemas, y comenzar una nueva vida en un país totalmente diferente al suyo, con otras tradiciones y costumbres, y con otro idioma.

Ruth y su familia llegaron a casa de una amiga que vivía en Charlottesville, VA. Después de algunos meses, Ruth se embaraza de su 3er hijo, a quien llamó Jesús. Sus hijas empezaron a estudiar y en solo seis meses aprendieron inglés. Para Ruth, resultaba difícil ayudarlas con la tarea, pues no sabía inglés, y aun cuando se auxiliaba del traductor del teléfono celular, le resultaba complicado traducir palabra por palabra. Fue así como Ruth decidió estudiar inglés en Literacy Volunteers. Hoy en día ella puede ayudar a su hijo Jesús, quien está en sexto grado; sin embargo, ella no se conformó solamente con aprender inglés, decidió obtener su GED y así poder tener mejores oportunidades de empleo. Su esposo Salomón ha ido aprendiendo Inglés con sus compañeros de trabajo en la construcción, la yarda, restaurante o donde le salga la oportunidad, ya que le gusta ganarse la vida honestamente. Como familia dan servicios en la Iglesia, trabajando con el ministerio de lectores, justicia y caridad IMPACT. Hoy en día, los hijos de Ruth colaboran como intérpretes tanto en la iglesia como en la escuela o donde se les solicite, y siguiendo con el ejemplo de sus padres, ellos se esfuerzan diariamente en la escuela para ser buenos estudiantes.

Milagro y Deborah son beneficiarias del programa DACA, otorgado por el presidente Obama. En la actualidad, Milagro está estudiando el segundo año de universidad con una beca del 60%. Ella ha trabajado mucho para conseguir este tipo de apoyos, de los que destacan la beca de Emily Couric, la cual ella ganó en el 2015, y también ayuda del PVCC. Actualmente, estudia para ser maestra. Por otro lado, Deborah, está a punto de graduarse de la preparatoria, trabajando en las aplicaciones para las universidades y alcanzar su sueño de llegar a ser profesional.

Además Ruth obtuvo en el 2015 un diploma que la acredita como "Promotora de Salud" de Charlottesville-CHW el cual le permite colaborar y ser parte de un equipo de voluntarios con el Departamento de Salud y con doctores y estudiantes de medicina de UVA. Esto le permite ayudar a la comunidad Latina de Charlottesville.

El más reciente desafío que se ha presentado para Ruth, es la elección como presidente de Donald Trump, quien amenaza con una deportación masiva, sin embargo ella y su familia se muestran muy agradecidos y optimistas por todo lo que este país y sus personas les han brindado de forma incondicional. Su historia de migración hacia lo desconocido es una inspiración de que no importan los obstáculos que en la vida se presenten siempre se puede salir adelante con los sueños que uno se proponga en la vida.

Cómo respondieron nuestros jueces y lectores…

"¡Qué mujer increíble! Debe haber sido aterrador comenzar una nueva vida con hijos pequeños en un país extranjero. Pero como tu historia muestra tan elocuentemente, Ruth tenía un poderoso sueño de una vida mejor que la guiaba cada día mientras trabajaba tan duro. ♥ Ella y su esposo establecieron fuertes modelos a seguir para sus hijas, que ahora están esparciendo sus propias alas en el camino hacia el éxito. ♥ Tu historia completa el ciclo de la narrativa al describir cómo Ruth ahora está ayudando a otros latinos a alcanzar sus sueños. ♥ Tu historia está imbuida de amor, respeto y honor por esta extraordinaria mujer. El éxito de Ruth y su familia en América es inspirador. Espero que nada obstaculice sus vidas aquí."

Challenge into Change

Biografía:

María Godoy es originaria de El Salvador, donde estudió para convertirse en docente de educación media superior. Se considera a sí misma como una persona emprendedora y entusiasta, que disfruta trabajar arduamente para alcanzar los objetivos que se plantea. Es una mujer que da lo mejor de sí misma en cada una de las situaciones que se le presentan día a día. María disfruta de la compañía de las personas y le gusta contagiarlas con su optimismo y buen humor; quienes la conocen saben que es una mujer dedicada y amorosa, prueba de ello es la hermosa familia que ella y su esposo has logrado formar bajo los mismos valores que rigen su vida. Dentro de sus actividades favoritas, encontramos aquellas que le ayudan a mejorar su salud, como correr o nadar, sin embargo también dedica un espacio de su día a la cocina donde realiza los más exquisitos platillos que asombran a su familia.

A Family that Migrates to the US

(English translation from Spanish)
(Names changed to protect privacy)

Maria Godoy

In 2005, Ruth migrated to the United States in search of the American dream along with her husband Salomán and their daughters: Milagro and Deborah. When she arrived, she had to face several challenges, from the most basic ones such as finding a place to live, enroll her daughters in school, get a job, among others. She had to solve these problems quickly so she could begin a new life in a country that was totally different from hers with different traditions and customs.

Ruth and her family arrived at her friend's house in Charlottesville, VA. After a few months, Ruth got pregnant with her 3rd child, who she and her husband named Jesus. Their daughters started school and it took them only six months to learn to speak English. For Ruth, it was difficult to help them with homework, as she was not familiar with the language and even though they used the cell phone's translator; it was very complicated for them to translate word by word. It was in this moment when Ruth decided to study English with the help of the Literacy Volunteers of Charlottesville. Nowadays she is able to help Jesus with his homework who, by the way, is currently in the sixth grade. At this time she was not satisfied by just speaking English, therefore she decided to get her GED and get better job opportunities. Ruth has used what she has learned to support her husband Salomán with the language, he has been learning English by speaking with his co-workers at the construction business, gardening, at the restaurant or wherever he has an opportunity to work, as he likes to have an honest lifestyle. As a family they do service at Church, working with the Ministry of Readers, Justice and Charity IMPACT. Nowadays, their children collaborate as interpreters as well as in church as in school or wherever their services are requested, they are following their parents example, they work really hard daily in school to obtain good grades.

Milagro and Deborah are beneficiaries of the DACA program, granted by President Obama. Currently, Milagro is a sophomore student at her college with a 60% scholarship. She has worked hard to obtain this kind of support, of which Emily Couric's scholarship stands out, which she won in 2015 and she also receives help from PVCC. She is currently studying to become a Teacher. On the other side, Deborah is about to graduate from High School, she is currently filling out college applications and someday achieve her dream of becoming a professional.

Additionally, in 2015 Ruth obtained a diploma accrediting her as a Charlottesville-CHW "Health Promoter", which allows her to collaborate and be part of a team of volunteers with the Department of Health and with doctors and UVA medical students. This allows her to help the Latino community in Charlottesville.

The latest challenge for Ruth and her family is Donald Trump's election as president, who threatens a massive deportation, but she and her family are feeling very grateful and optimistic because of all that this country and its people have provided in an unconditional way. Her story of migration to the unknown is an inspiration that no matter what obstacles in life are presented you can always get ahead with the dreams that one proposes in life

---

How our judges and readers responded...

What an amazing woman! It must have been frightening to start a whole new life with young children in a foreign land. But as your story so eloquently shows, Ruth had a powerful dream of a better life that guided her every day as she worked so hard. ♥ She and her husband were strong role models for their daughters, who are now spreading their own wings on the way to success. ♥ You bring the narrative full circle, describing how Ruth is now helping other Latinos achieve their dreams. ♥ Your story is imbued with love, respect, and honor for this remarkable woman. Ruth and her family's success in America is inspiring. I hope nothing hinders their lives here.

BIO:

Maria Godoy was born in El Salvador, where she studied to become a high school teacher. She considers herself to be an enterprising and enthusiastic person who enjoys working hard to achieve her goals. She is a woman who gives the best of herself in each of the situations of her everyday life. Maria enjoys being with people as well as sharing with them her optimism and sense of humor; those who know her agree that she is a dedicated and loving woman, proof of which is the beautiful family that she and her husband have raised under the same values that govern their lives. Among her favorite activities she enjoys those that help her improve her health, such as running or swimming, but she also dedicates a space of her day to cook the most exquisite meals that astonish her family.

I WASN'T GOOD ENOUGH

Tanya Denise Gordon

I wasn't good enough to sing on stage

I wasn't good enough as your child

I wasn't good enough as a student

I wasn't good enough on my birthday

I wasn't good enough on Christmas

I wasn't good enough as a mother

I wasn't good enough as a lover

I wasn't get enough to be loved

I wasn't good enough as a witness

I wasn't good enough at physical fitness

I wasn't good enough in church

I wasn't good enough as a sister

I wasn't good enough as a visitor

I wasn't good as an owner

I was good enough as their auntie

I wasn't good enough at anything I ever tried

I wasn't good enough that's why they all lied

I wasn't good enough no matter what I tried

I wasn't good enough that why I always cried

I wasn't good enough that's why I finally let go and kept everything I felt inside

I wasn't good enough that's why I died

But now you say that she is good enough now that I am no longer alive.

How our judges and readers responded...

The repetitive structure of this poem drives home the pain of the way the author has felt judged negatively by others. ♥ *Whereas the author once "kept everything I felt inside," she has now put her feelings into the world by writing them down, an admirable first step toward finding healing.* ♥ *You are more than good enough!* ♥ *Thank you for writing about your feelings.*

BIO:

I am currently a PVCC student and I am taking Administrative Assistant classes my focus is to work in a doctor's office. I have recently been reintroduced to my love of writing poetry and writing stories. I currently reside in Greene County but I am originally from Orange County. I have plans in the fall to go back into college at American National College in College to take a refresher course in Medical Billing and Coding. I am the single mother of four children who I have struggled to raise alone and I see and am witness to those struggles and consequences every day. People do not realize especially families that it takes a village to raise a child and I asked my village for help and there was no one to help everyone was too busy, no one realized that if I failed in my fight for my children in raising them the right way and teaching them the values that they would need in the world that they failed my children as well because they did not help me with them, that is why I say consequences of raising my children alone.

Challenge into Change

Bits N Pieces

Sekina L. Greene

Praising The Lord with all of my heart and soul, I'm a women who serve The Lord attends church every Sunday and Tuesday for bible study, and every third Thursday for choir rehearsal, I am in the class for ministry training, a teacher in the children church every 3rd and 4th Sunday, Minister every 3-6 months The Word of God to the kids in the detention home. There is so much excitement when a child who lost their way, find The Lord during their days while incarceration to takes a stand to be saved and set from there ways that caused them to be in that place for the moment. My life today is serve The Glory of God, I could have not prayed for a better life, if it wasn't for my grannie who made me go to church when I was a kid, showing me the reason to attend church, as a kid I thought it was great just going to the candy store after service to get penny candy, I truly Thank her always.

My life started with me growing up with a dysfunctional family background, we may all relate to having this in our families, living a life with not knowing for sure who's house or where we going to live, depending on how our mother was feeling and how others felt about her, we would bounce around from an Aunt's house, neighbors' house then back to grandma's house. I'll share Bits N Pieces of my younger years when I was introduced to my father, It was a sunny afternoon I was told that a man that drove pass in a white van was my father and I asked if it's true could I go see him, waiting for my grandmother to give me answer, made me feel anxious in knowing if this is true was overwhelming, I rode my aunt's bike to find out if this was true, I had the courage to ask the man who drove the white van, who was putting cement on the ground, I said " hello, are you my dad?", he looked at me and smile and said yes, your name is Sekina!... I was so HAPPY, smiling it started me asking more and more questions. Years of building a long lasting relationship with the man in the white van, it all shattered into pieces after the death of his life, months turn into years, we truly didn't get a chance to bond like father to daughter, he taught me so much valuable lessons in life that I keep close and near, learning how to fix cars was the best gift he gave me, I would write letters to him and never mailed it, I have a notebook filled with letters telling him how I am and how much I miss him, his voice was very loud in my head, once I see his picture I start crying, reflecting on the day January 24th 2005, right after his grandson's birthday.

How our judges and readers responded…

There is so much joy and sadness contained in this piece. ♥ *It really captures a full spectrum of the intensity of human experience.* ♥ *Your use of detail is beautiful—the sunny day, the white van. I can picture these moments; you really make them come alive.*

BIO:

Sekina here, and I come to you with a humble heart, stepping out of faith by sharing some small clips about my journey before I became a child of God, it all started with not having a true direction in life, when I lost what I thought was my only hope (My Dad), was my only answer I soon found out, there was Hope in God. As a teenage mom, struggling through life holding on to the rails of a fast-moving roller coaster. I am a proud mother of 3 adults and reside in Virginia Beach for 18 years, I am glad I took the courage to submit my story to show how faith works. Thank you again for allowing me to share my journey walk into my newness.

Challenge into Change

SHE IS MY MOM!
Waheda Haidari

Yes! My mom, who inspires me in my life the most. She is a hard-working woman. She is the mother of four children who raised them alone in poverty, loneliness, and complex problems. I remember the cold days of our life when my mom had to stitch traditional pillowcases and get some money to feed her children. I grew up in Pakistan for fifteen years sometimes happy, sometimes sad, sometimes with love and sometimes with hatred. I went to school there until my junior year but predicting a dark future with all of the impossible hopes, at least in that situation. I loved to watch Indian dramas, but I didn't have TV or anything else to entertain myself. If I played with other girls they were always fighting with each other, so I didn't need more because I already had in my house. I couldn't play with boys because they would tease me due to my gender. I went to my mom and complained about everything, about that she can't provide us anything, about why are we poor. Why I can't be like my friends rich, happy, and free? But she was always giving me hope about future that I should study and provide all my needs by myself. She was stitching days and nights to gather money to buy us TV. I saw her a lot of times when needle poked inside her fingers, but she continued stitching. You might think I didn't have a dad, I actually had, he was in Russia. He couldn't make much income to send home a lot every month, as he says. I just saw him twice for two months in that entire fifteen years plus one year living in Afghanistan which is sixteen years. So my mom was a dad and a mom for me. Finally, she saved ten thousand Pakistani rupees equivalent to a hundred USD. It doesn't seem quite a lot of money but it was for us. Eventually, she bought us a TV. Oh! you can't believe how much I was happy. when the TV was set, for the first time I took the remote control and started changing the channels. It felt so good, I did not get tired because I could watch my favorite dramas in my own TV! I thanked my mom so much! She is my hero. She inspires me that I can achieve my goals maybe not soon but later. I remember the days that my mom stood against my uncles and grandpa to not deprive me of further education. My mom faced difficulties of couldn't bearing a son, then being not educated, having many girls and more. But let me tell you, I believe she is a good wife for my dad, the best mother for us, and the best and bravest woman in the world. The unfortunate is that she couldn't raise her voice, But I promise her I will be her voice because she is my mom!

How our judges and readers responded...

There are so many beautiful stories here and it is amazing that this piece tells them in so few words. The story of living poor in Pakistan, the story of youthful friendships, the story of mother's sewing, the story of the TV, and the story of dreams for a better life. ♥ *The author's mother would be so proud of this writing because the author is not only using their voice in ways that their mother could not, but they are also showing the world her loving and invigorating spirit.*

BIO:

My name is Waheda Haidari. I am living in Charlottesville. I am in my junior year at Charlottesville High School. I came to the United States in 2014. Before I was in Pakistan for fifteen years, then I moved to Afghanistan and lived there for a year. I love to write story.

Challenge into Change

Pray Your Way Up

Peggy Jean Hatton

In the book of my life, the page yesterday is over. I have accepted my past with no regrets. When I look back over my life, tears flow because if it hadn't been for God being on my side, I wouldn't be here to share my story, to spread hope, joy and love to the world. Thank goodness, I didn't get stuck but moved past my circumstances when I was diagnosed with my first brain tumor.

I say first, because there was a second time around, and that was a severe blow that overpowered me and almost put me under. I was a single woman working on my job in the medical field with no expectation of bad news when I begin experiencing severe headaches and knew something was wrong. An MRI was ordered, and my peaceful life was impacted significantly when the doctor called me at work and gave me the results.

She said, "Ms. Hatton, you have a brain tumor." "What?" I cried," wanted to scream to the rooftop. I had to hold on to my control because I was at work. The first time that came to my mind was, "I am going to die." Just like that, my life was shattered. It hurt so bad; I was like an uncontrollable child that won't stop crying. I kept asking, "Why me, Lord?" The holy spirit said, "Peggy, why not you?" "Don't be discouraged."

"I will always be with you like the footsteps in the sand." God granted me peace of mind to accept what was, strength and comfort to go on and have the surgery. When I woke up after the brain tumor was surgically removed, I found I was given my second chance at life. Even though I woke up temporary blind, I knew God had given me a second chance, making me the head not the tail. I went back to work after six months. I never had the same capability as I had before surgery. I had a heart of gratitude.

Eight years later, my life was disrupted when I started having headaches again. I knew the brain tumor had returned. An MRI was taken and revealed another brain tumor. I had been working in the medical field for 28 years. I had major complications that caused me to become disabled. My job was all that I knew. Instead of retiring as I had planned, I was without hope for my future.

I was forced into the wilderness, searching for solutions. I didn't know who I was anymore. When financial hardship hit, it left me living in poverty. I read my bible and kept my faith. God didn't promise day without pain, laughter without sorrow, sun without rain, but he did promise strength for the day and comfort for our tears and light for the way.

Today, I don't know my future prognosis, but I know the God that I serve. I fear not, because I found peace in God.

How our judges and readers responded...

This is an incredible story of faith and perseverance. Your strength and faith infuses this piece with hope and reassurance. ♥ *What a moving story of strength through faith. You have found sustenance where many would feel abandoned.*

BIO:

When I look back over my life tears flow, because if it hadn't been for God on my side, I wouldn't be here to share my story.

Challenge into Change

Boots, Boobs and Mojo

Shaaron Honeycutt

I stand propped up against a wall, needing its support and wondering how much energy I have left and it's only 12:30 - barely afternoon. My friend Cathy has brought me to my favorite consignment shop to find shirts that button up, now that I cannot take them on and off over my head. I am struggling to find the afterglow of having my cumbersome and uncomfortable drains out. I am 2 weeks post op from a radical bilateral mastectomy. My spirits are at an all-time low. I put on a good face but it's a ruse and takes energy I just don't have right now. I stand in the window of time where I am lucid but the pain meds are wearing off and know I'm going to need to get horizontal very soon. I have no money because I haven't worked for the past 3 weeks, and being self-employed has many perks, but paid sick leave is not one of them. Frankly I'm not sure how much worse my life can get (Don't hear that Universe! I'm NOT asking for you to show me…). I find a couple of shirts that suit me and am "playing" in the high-end designer area. I am biding my time for Cathy to finish her browsing and shopping, knowing there's nothing there I can afford even with Cathy's generous donation of her consignment dollars on file with the shop. The women know me there, I stop in with some regularity as most less affluent fashionistas do… trolling the cast offs of the more well-heeled, literally. One of the woman asks me how I am and I actually tell her, as I have no capacity to filter my experience right now. I look at the designer boots and shoes admiringly. "What size are you?" She asks. I reply "about a 7"… "hold on a minute" when she returns from a disappearance to the back room with a box and opens it, and I swear the sun came out as though from behind a cloud, and possibly angels hummed a note or two, because there are the most spectacular black Fiorentini + Baker boots, still wrapped in tissue and have obviously never, ever worn. I hold my breath, knowing that they won't fit and therefore I'll have the perfect excuse not to buy them. And, like the proverbial Cinderella, they slide onto my feet as though custom-made. At that moment, I felt like

Challenge into Change

things might turn out ok. The boots symbolized to me something greater than my poor, sad, suffering, bruised and beat-up body: hope.

The cosmos was returning my mojo to me, all that I was and could still be, in the form of some stunning and ass-kicking boots.

I immediately considered them my "bon voyage to boobs boots" and gifted myself. Maybe with them on I can "float a little above this difficult world" (to quote Mary Oliver) and do it with STYLE.

How our judges and readers responded…

Powerful. Reader senses that this writer will face her future with confidence and energy. ♥ *The sense of humor and tireless spirit of the protagonist is contagious in this story. We understand the pain and tragedy she has faced, yet laugh with her as she finds beauty in her everyday life.* ♥ *Her perspective brings strength to those who read her words.*

BIO:

Shaaron's deep and challenging life experiences allow her to bring a unique perspective into her writing and her yoga teaching. Continually inspired by her those around her, Shaaron strives to, in turn, uplift and challenge those she comes into contact with to move beyond their perceived limitations and manifest the greatness that is inherent in all of us. Shaaron has a sharp wit and shows how the gift of humor can be shared while incorporating it into her writing and each class she teaches, enabling the "medicine" and challenge of personal growth and change to go "down" with ease and joy.

Challenge into Change

INSANITY

j

Insanity. Doing the same thing over and over and expecting different results.

I've chanted these words to myself, repeatedly, over the last 30 years. A reminder. A mantra.

Serenity – to accept the things I cannot change, courage to change the things I can, and the wisdom to know the difference. These words usually follow.

They are diabolically opposed, these phrases. Yet today, they are both alive and breathing in me every day.

The insanity. It has run rampant through my life. Repeatedly reacting to situations the same way.

The situations. Most stem from childhood, learning not to "feel", not to express any emotions that are other than happiness. Stuffing the feelings because others have taught that they are wrong, that if expressed, will cause others to be unhappy. Hardening the heart, not trusting people, situations, feelings, or myself.

Where did that lead? Alcoholism, domestic abuse, spouse's infidelity, divorce, sudden death of a child, a child in and out of treatment for mental illness, and ultimately deciding that I could not trust or depend on anyone, or myself, for anything. That feelings needed to be shuttered away and I slowly built a protective wall around myself.

Insanity led me to continually attempt to be vulnerable, attempt to trust, to accept things which were not healthy for me – physically or emotionally. All with the wrong people. Insanity led me to continually base my worth on what others thought of me. Always thinking, if only I do this for them, then he/she will love me, be happy, treat

130   *Challenge into Change*

me well. The result? Feeling unworthy of love, unworthy of kindness, unworthy of happiness. Unworthy. And unworthiness leads to lack of self-care. I don't deserve to do things for myself – I'm not making others happy by my repeated attempts to try to be who they want me to be, so how can I be worthy of doing something good and nice and healthy for me?

I grasp at serenity – I have a permanent reminder that this is my goal. The insanity still holds on tight, it's insidious. Evil. Relentless.

And today. These past few months have been a reminder that yes, the insanity is alive and well. A fiancé. A betrayal. Repeating the past, hoping against hope that this time it will be different. Insanity.

However, now there is a light. The serenity, the acceptance, the courage and the wisdom are peaking through. A therapist that insists on self-care. Which turns into breathing, rewiring my thinking, yoga, walking, meds, more breathing, massages, writing, working to discover who I am (not who others think I am or insist that I be), and yet again, more and more breathing.

Serenity.
Accept the things I cannot change. Other people.
Courage to change the things I can. Me.
Wisdom to know the difference. Ah, the toughest of all.

It is a daily struggle and the difference now is I have HOPE. Hope and willingness to take care of me, learn about me. Love me? Soon, I hope. Serenity.

Challenge into Change

How our judges and readers responded...

It takes a lot of courage to be so direct about tragedy and trauma—thank you for sharing this intimate story. ♥ *Really interesting contrast between "insanity" and "serenity." I can imagine these as dueling forces in your life, and I hope you can move toward your version of serenity.*

BIO:

A mom of 4 semi-adults - one of whom lives forever in my heart. A working professional who sometimes wonders how she has achieved so much. But most of all, a woman who is learning to be brave, strong, and a warrior.

Discovering My Calling, Securing My Future
Valerie R. Jackson

I did the math: 10 short years to Social Security benefits, 5 failed career choices, and zero dollars in a 401(k). With the looming prospect of a position as an elderly Wal-Mart greeter on the horizon, I needed to come up with a plan. I needed more than a good job; I needed to find my calling.

If I had a lick of sense I would have given up, trudged my way to retirement through a series of dead-end jobs, and spent my golden years mastering the art of the tiny budget. Every stress-inducing life change in the past seven years – a bad divorce, a cross-country move, exhausting work schedules, single-parenthood, and my descent into poverty-level wages – would have been enough to make anybody conclude life was simply out to get them.

I scolded myself. Over 50? No marketable skills? No resources? You can't build a business on that! Besides, you're way too old for a career change. And remember that year of college you took just when you were getting divorced? The one you're still paying for? Another student loan is out of the question!

But, as I recalled my previous determination to complete my education, I thought of something. When the long-deferred opportunity came to take my senior year, I told myself: "Look. In another year, you're going to be 46, anyway. Do you want to be 46 with a degree? Or 46 without a degree?" In other words, my future starts now!

My current challenge is to build a career for myself and do it without any money. There would be no college courses for re-training and no start-up funds. I had to work with whatever skills and resources I already possessed and keep an eye out for anything and everything that was free. I had to become self-taught, and I had to make a little bit go a very long way.

Challenge into Change

Having acquired a multitude of almost-marketable skills throughout my work life, in the end I simply returned to something I learned in 10th grade: typing. Okay, it's called keyboarding these days, and I had to repackage what I was offering to meet modern needs. But I already owned a computer with a word processing program and that was all I needed to get started. Internet service? Free at the library. Accounting and billing? Free online. Business training? SCORE was there for me. Start-up funds? If I could just get $25 a month into a bank account, the state of Virginia would match it.

When my first potential client asked if I could not only edit their manuscript but take it all the way to publication, I cheerily said, "Sure!" Then I scrambled to learn those skills before they sent me the job. Learning to write, edit, and publish a book of my own became one of many self-designed training programs. Success also reassured me that, with determination, I could accomplish anything I needed to accomplish. Even securing my future.

How our judges and readers responded…

Yours is a great story of "pulling yourself up by your bootstraps!" When people read your story they will be inspired to keep on trying even when past experience has left them discouraged. ♥ Determined, strong, self-reliant woman—and a clear writer. She showed what we might consider to be of little value as very valuable to her. She used these "free" resources to add value to her life. ♥ In this piece, the author uses a conversational style to win over the reader and engages us in a discourse on how human spirit and ingenuity can overcome even the most intransigent of economic challenges.

Challenge into Change

BIO:

Valerie R. Jackson is a Virginia transplant from pretty much everywhere, having moved to Charlottesville from Abilene, TX. She is a lifelong artist and writer with a wide range of interests. For the past year, she has brought many of her skills together to start her own transcription business. She has three children and (almost!) four grandchildren. Currently she is married to Johnny Jackson Sr and living in Louisa, VA.

Long Way Home

Eilise Johnson

As I watch my father fade away with tears in my eyes. I have to find
time away so I can have my cries.

I look at him and I often wonder what it is he sees. I just cannot
help but to think what a horrible disease.

I tell my father I will always pray to be able to see him through I
know you don't remember everyone but they remember you.

Some days he has a sense of humor as funny as can be. We smile,
and we laugh and talk about the good times we use to see.

He lived his life with so much integrity, grace, and class. I am so
very sad for him that his memories did not last.

And as I say my prayer for him it is that he can be as healthy and as
happy till the lord sets him free.

How our judges and readers responded...

A very nicely written poem. ♥ *You capture your thoughts and feelings about
your father's illness in such concise language.* ♥ *I'm sure your father would
appreciate this wonderful tribute.*

BIO:

Eilise's field is Business Administration, and has been a family care-giver since 2011. She is a new writer and have been inspired to write to bring awareness to Lewy Body Dementia. Eilise received a Business Management degree in 1984 from Shaw University, Raleigh, NC. Eilise wrote her first article, *"Living with Lewy Body Dementia / Parkinson's"* and it appeared in the Vinegar Hill Society summer issue. Eilise has also been inspired to patent an invention in the healthcare industry. Eilise resides in Charlottesville, VA.

Birth Trauma Is Real
Brianne Kirkpatrick

These things are hard to hold at the same time, gratefulness and anger. Inside, I'm at war against myself. Grateful for the lives of my children, entrusted to me for care. One minute I'm shaking a fist at the sky for what it took to get them born and all of us home from the hospital safely. The next I feel only gratitude. I'm still not "over" it. Almost six years and nine years later, memories from my childbirths are burned deep. Without warning, any one of the moments can replay through my mind. Some triggers can be prepared for, like the annual trek to the gynecology office. Some can't be, though. Seeing an ambulance drive by. Walking past the diaper aisle. Random "maternity care" emails that still arrive from the hospital where I delivered, even though my baby is in Kindergarten and I now live states away.

How can I be angry at these people at the hospital, who were my colleagues at the time, for letting something happen that changed me for the better? How can I feel regret but also the deepest sense of luck for having had the opportunity to confront death, and survive? How do I reconcile knowing these people were human with feeling *they are not supposed to make their medical mistakes when I am their patient?*

It has taken six years, four counselors, journaling, and conversations with multitudes. My husband, my sisters, other families, friends. "You have PTSD," one counselor finally spoke. "Birth trauma." Yeah, I know, I thought. I have every book about birth trauma I can find sitting on my bookshelf. But...but my babies and I are okay. And healthy. *Why is that not enough?* And so I eventually found my way to a special therapy for PTSD survivors. A few months of this therapy - called EMDR - has helped me process what years of talk therapy could not.

For six years, I've lived my life mostly moving on, only a part of me suspended. In time. In disbelief. In a fight with myself to let go of the memories and resolve the anger. I had to allow myself to get angry before I could move on. It is more difficult to get mad at people who are your friends and acquaintances, which means getting past the anger to healing is challenging, too.

Fear of loss. This is what it all boils down to now. The grief and the anger are being peeled back to reveal what lies at the center. Having been faced with the reality that is the risk of loss present in every pregnancy and childbirth, I take a step back. The naiveté that was present in my first pregnancy is gone and won't return. In its place would be a tempered excitement. Anticipation and joy mixed with fear and doubt.

The extra chair at the dining table sits empty. I look at it and imagine what that little face would have looked like. Big, round, blue eyes, like my other two? Hair that curls? Do I risk all the great things I have going right now, risk my presence on this Earth, to find out what that little face looks like?

What *will* that little face look like?

Challenge into Change

How our judges and readers responded...

Yours is a moving story. The tension that you describe between gratefulness and anger is easy to imagine. I hope that the empty chair at your table can be filled. ♥ *There is power and fortitude here, and self-awareness. Immediate and unsettling—unexpected conclusion.* ♥ *The writer does an excellent job sharing how one of the most beautiful acts on God's earth—giving birth—can also bring with it pain, hurt, sorrow, etc. It appears she's saying having the children/giving birth to these beings and what they bring to her life far outweigh the risks. The question of how we move on after trauma is at the center of this inspiring reflection.* ♥ *Its prose cuts deep in its expression of the scars that can form based on experience, yet its conclusion gives hope for moving beyond these experiences to pursue new life and dreams.*

BIO:

Brianne Kirkpatrick is a mother of two, a genetic counselor, and a writer. She lives with her husband and children in Crozet, Virginia and owns and runs a private tele-consultancy on DNA testing called WatershedDNA.

Dear Aunt Mary,
Nina Knight

Dec. 2016

Dear Aunt Mary,

I know that you aren't around to hear what I have to say, but somehow that just doesn't matter. To say that the two years since you died were not full of challenges into changes is an understatement. I need you to know what is going on with me and how much I miss you.

It was about the time that you fell ill that I picked up the phone in hopes that I could spend a week or so with you. Shawn and I were going through a rough patch and I needed space and some special time with just the two of us. Unfortunately, you were too ill for that to happen and it wasn't long before you made your journey to Heaven. Things between Shawn and myself didn't improve and I am now divorced. As a coping strategy, I changed my last name to Knight. Nina Knight has a nice ring to it and I wanted to honor your mother by choosing her maiden name, because I loved her as much as you did.

I do want you to know about the amazing support I have gotten from the folks at Region Ten. My case manager was able to find me a place to live on short notice and when that place didn't work out, she found another spot that is a better fit. The walls of my room are decorated with my creative efforts, including a picture of a frog so you are never far from my thoughts. Also, a cheerful worker named Annie visits once a week to go over budgeting and other such matters. To say that I could not have made it without them is an understatement.

The biggest news in the Ellis household is that Anne-Marie is now one week away from delivering boy number two! This means that you have a total of 3 grandbabies, counting John Priester's Addison. I am enjoying being an aunt to Frances' Sammy, now four months. I

Challenge into Change

can hardly wait for him to be old enough for stories at Aunt Nina's house.

Please know that you are deeply missed by lots of folks, not just myself. By the way, I do hope that you had as John Priester said on the night before me wedding "Good Luck On The Bumpy Road to Heaven."

Love,

Nina Knight

How our judges and readers responded...

I am deeply touched by your letter — so personal and tender, revealing your profound connection with your family. There is joy and gratitude in what you write, but also a vulnerability that takes great courage to put down on paper. ♥ *The decision to take your grandmother's maiden name shows a woman claiming her identity, her power.* ♥ *The detail of a picture of a frog on your wall is a charming touch, like a secret shared between you and Mary. She is, indeed, never far away.* ♥ *You have written an inspiring letter to your aunt. You have been able to use all the help you have received. Not everyone can do this.*

BIO:

A recent divorcee, Nina Knight has an amazing attitude towards life and all of its challenges into changes. Her favorite color is purple (the color of royalty) and her favorite movie is Star Wars. If pressed to choose her favorite characters, it's the three gentlemen robots: C3PO, R2D2, and BB8. The walls of her new room on Spruce Street are decorated with all sorts of her creative efforts as her other passion is coloring. Nina is also doing a bit of creative writing and hopes to one day publish a book of her own. One of her favorite quotes is "Shoot for the moon, even if you miss, you will land amongst the stars."

May
Audrey Kocher

As we walk along the lane, the sky is exceptionally blue, clouds white, billowy. I reach to touch them. Petals of May flowers give fullness to each blossom. I see the whole patch and separate plants at the same time. I never forget.

While Mom delivers grandmother's laundry, my brother, sister and I join cousins and other town kids in play already underway. Girls gather flowers for Snow White's wedding. In service to the Queen, boys appear with bows and arrows, intent on shooting Snow White. Missing her, I am hit. Flossie, who has so many children she doesn't know what to do and lives in a house that looks like a shoe, clutches and comforts me.

After surgery, both eyes are bandaged. When the bandage over one eye is removed, I see clearly. I am confined; no one checks on me. Needing to pee, I climb out the crib, nearly falling from weakness. My parents visit when possible. Others aren't allowed. I'm on my own.

Once healed, I'm taken to an office. The desk is covered with velvet cases containing square sections; each holding an artificial eye. Big, small, various shapes and colors, they stare in different directions. Samples are painfully pushed into my eye socket while the lids are held open. Drops moisten the socket and lubricate the dry, hard discs. Crying isn't tolerated. Later, my father argues about payment of bills with the father of the shooter. I don't matter. I feel responsible.

Asked if I'm the one whose eye was shot out, disgust shows on their faces. Indicating they can hardly tell which eye is injured, they add "it's the left one." I stop looking at people. Unlike Cinderella's prince, dates don't search the realm for me. Have town folk anticipated this when they collect $25 for my education?

Challenge into Change

Counseling isn't available. Can 7 year olds put feelings into words? Anyway, no one asks. Encouraging words aren't given beyond those of the friendly hospital housekeeper who is positive I will like wearing glasses. As an adult, I try counselling. Without guidance, I can't begin. The psychologist dozes. I never return.

I recall fairy tales: work hard, overcome adversity, marry a handsome prince, live happily ever after. I compete college, make lifelong friends, and have a fulfilling career. Patients provide more courage and joy than assistance I provide them.

Surgeries improve my appearance. Occasionally, complements include "you have pretty blue eyes!" Writing about her adoption experience, my daughter states how much we look alike. Happy tears flow.

My daughter asks what her life would be like if she hadn't adopted. Asking myself what my life would be like if reenacting a fairy tale 65 years ago hadn't been interrupted, I have no answer.

May is still beautiful even if clouds look flat. I remember the world is three dimensional. I no longer try to touch clouds. I still caress, examine my world and feelings to understand their fullness. I matter to me, to my daughter, to others.

How our judges and readers responded…

The ethereal voice of this piece thrusts readers into the speaker's reality, urging us at once to see through her eyes and to see her. This seems a perfect request as we watch the speaker grow and overcome obstacles. ♥ *This story is beautiful, lyrical, and inspiring. You faced a terrible challenge, but clearly you found that you had the inner resources to lead a truly fulfilling life.*

BIO:

Raised in poverty, we did not have running water or an indoor bath room until I was a teen. I graduated from Penn State and completed graduate studies at Case Western Reserve, the first in my family to do so. As I look back, it has taken 65 years to work through the aftermath of an accident when I was 7 years old. What follows is that effort.

Changing through Dream Work
Phyllis R. Koch-Sheras, PhD

Being on time has been an issue for me forever. Being a psychologist and a mediator, I have worked on it in many venues, leading to an expanded awareness of the issue and some limited progress. It was not until I worked on the following dream that I had during a Tibetan Buddhist retreat recently, however, that I had a real breakthrough in being on time.

"Someone tells me that one of the retreatants has been arrested and will likely be put to death at 7 a.m. unless a petition for an extension is submitted before then. It is already too late, but I decided to try and submit it anyway. I feel worried, responsible and guilty. Suddenly I realize that this is a dream, and I can change it. I don't have to be late!"

I worked on this dream using the method I have created called "dream language". It involves rephrasing the dream in the present tense, like telling a story, and a focusing on everything in the dream as being parts of one self, created by the dreamer. This is based on the philosophy that all aspects of life exist in every human being, positive and negative. So anything that appears in a dream not only represents your perception of the people, places, objects, and occurrences in your walking life, but also parts of you.

After the retreat, I worked on the dream with my "dream work partner" with whim I work on dreams on a regular basis. We always get messages from the dream about some changes or actions to take into or waking life. I got a message from the "retreatant part of me" to pay attention to the impact of being late on my health and on the feelings of others, especially my husband. I resolved to discuss the issue with him and make promises about being on time. I did so as soon as I got home and have been on time for most events we participate in together! The time of 7:00 in the morning was when the first practice of the day occurred during my retreat, a time that was a continual challenge for me to make. I got a message from the "petition part of me" to be resolute about my promise and intention to be on time – and to realize that while it is urgent, it is not "too late" to make significant changes to my behavior. Out of this, I created some strategies, like leaving more space between events that I schedule to allow me to be more relaxed and on time. While still a challenge, I have been on time to the 7 a.m. retreat practices and most other events in my life since then.

I hope that sharing my dream will motivate and help you to work on your dreams. We spend nearly one-third of our life asleep, with a significant amount of that time in the dream state. Let's not waste that valuable time!

How our judges and readers responded...

This piece is both aesthetically dreamy and inventively instructive. Asking your readers to consider their dream selves offers them a great power—a life changing ability to rethink their actions and their histories. ♥ *Thank you for writing about your success with dream work. Being chronically late is a problem that affects relationships.*

BIO:

Phyllis R. Koch-Sheras, PhD, is a clinical psychologist and author, living and working in Charlottesville since 1974. She has co-authored several books, including *The Dream Sourcebook, Couple Power Therapy* and *Lifelong Love*. Currently, she is writing a musical entitled "Therapy: the Musical." She has been involved in Tibetan Buddhist studies and practice at Serenity Ridge in Nelson County for over 20 years. Phyllis is also a professional opera singer and watercolor artist. She is married and has two grown children.

Challenge into Change

Never. Give. Up.
Krista

My pain started over the winter. It stayed through the summer. After work one day, I came home to an empty house. "Where is my family?" I sent a message to my then best friend knowing that my husband had planned to see her that day. Why wouldn't they want to see me too?

My blood turned to ice when I read her response. "The boys are playing and having fun here." Ice turned to hot rage as I drove an hour from my house to hers. Then I got another message telling me that my family had gone back home.

When I finally held my baby, he started to throw up, and he didn't stop for days. It felt like we had the flu. Valentine's Day was just a few days away. I waited for plans, chocolate, flowers, a card, candy, something, anything, but nothing happened. I got the kids to bed early and couldn't wait to spend some time with my Valentine, but he didn't even see me. He was in bed smiling and texting with my former best friend.

My heart was pierced with hopelessness. I showered my husband with rage. Then the silence came. For months. We went to a marriage counselor. We read The Seven Principals for Making Marriage Work. We went on dates and tried to 'turn toward each other,' but we actually fell further apart.

Several months later he left and told me he was no longer in love with me. But I refused to give up! I fought. For my marriage. For myself. For my kids. For our family to remain under one roof. I threw all of our wedding pictures into the front yard smashing the glass into pieces, telling the neighborhood the truth.

My husband returned. Finally, as the new school year began, I discovered the truth. My husband lowered his wall and allowed me to have access to his email. I started to sift through the rubble. 'Crisis' comes from the Greek word meaning 'to sift.' With the strength of my Greek ancestors I dug for treasure and truth.

My husband had been lying for months. His relationship with my former best friend continued well after I was told it had ended. I also discovered that there was another woman he had been going to see while I thought he was working.

What now? What do I do? He says he is sorry. He says that he loves me. Can I forgive him? It is so painful and hard, but I find an amazing grace through church, "Twas grace that taught my heart to fear, and grace my fears relieved. How precious did that grace appear, the hour I first believed."

It has been many more months now, and our marriage is still a work in progress. We are able to communicate much more openly and honestly now, and I think that even our kids know that no matter what we: Never. Give. Up.

How our judges and readers responded...

This is a beautiful story of courage, honesty, and grace. Love and an indomitable will to be a family permeate this piece. ♥ *Very touching. Your struggle to keep your marriage and family together is a valiant one.* ♥ *You are an example of courage and perseverance to us all.*

BIO:

Krista is a mom to two young boys. She teaches art now, but taught high school English before becoming a mother. She got a BA in English from James Madison University, and has taken education classes at Mary Baldwin College. She is a local and likes to spend her free time taking her boys outside to explore nature.

Challenge into Change

Presence
Meredith Largiader

"Relationship?"

"I am her mother."

The conversation ended after a few more questions. I put the phone down and squeezed my eyes shut. I replayed that simple statement in my mind: I am her mother. Present tense. During the call I had also confirmed my daughter's name and date of birth, as do all mothers countless times. I was doing it for the first time.

I was also doing it for the last time. The enormity of that fact was captured in the barely perceptible catch in the woman's breath when I stated that the date of her birth was the same as the date of her death.

Instead of making an appointment for her newborn checkup, I was finalizing arrangements for her cremation. The tidiness in our house remained unsullied by wayward miniscule socks. The continued normalcy of our schedule was a palpable reminder of what we had lost but never known. I had time for a shower, but that notion was as painful as my milk that sought in vain for a hungry mouth.

I am grateful that I have since had direct experience of the demands that a baby places on one's time and energy. Family, friends, and childcare can provide respite from those demands. But we cannot hand off our sorrow for someone else to bear for a few hours, and we cannot send it off to camp in the summer.

Society loves birth and babies. Strangers feel entitled to invade a pregnant woman's privacy. We do not feel the same about death and the dying. We stay away as if death were contagious. The intimate proximity of both extremes in our baby girl brought this contrast into sharp focus and was mirrored in the community: while it was so hard to be at home where her constant absence was a throbbing sore, being out meant repeatedly re-opening the wound and experiencing the fresh loss anew. Many who were eager to congratulate recoiled from the sting of the unexpected news. I found myself consoling others.

We need to practice living with death, and we need to learn to abide with sadness; this would ease our fears of both. The bereft are expected to get over things and move on, and we hide in our busy-ness from those feelings that are not fit for polite company. We can and should move forward after death, but we must bring our loved and lost with us, for we are not whole without them. Even knowing the sadness and regret I have about my daughter, I would rather have had the whole experience than none of it.

Those who stay away from the grieving complain that they do not know what to say. There is nothing to say. Just come, and be. Let me tell you about the time we had together. Let me tell you about my daughter.

How our judges and readers responded...

This piece challenges our conceptions of beginnings and endings by standing in a moment of great joy and incredible loss. It speaks beautifully and bravely to the realities of kinship, legacy, and motherhood. ♥ *You truly encourage us, as readers, to stretch ourselves and to build communities and to grow in our grief. The loss of a baby at birth is an experience people do not understand.* ♥ *Thank you for sharing your experience of this great loss with us.*

BIO:

Meredith Largiader lives in Charlottesville with her husband, two girls, and two cats.

You Are

Donna Lloyd

Domestic violence rocks a person's world.
It turns everything upside down.
It is a hurricane,
that blows the fiercest of winds.
It is a tsunami,
that slams you like a freight train.
It's an atomic bomb,
destroying everything you hold dear.

You wake up one day -
Your friends are gone.
Your family is gone.
But worst of all,
You are gone.

You were born with a light
burning bright - deep inside you.
It has always been there.
When the dark days come,
go and find this light.
Take hold of its hand.
You will do things you have
long since forgotten you could do.
You have the power.
You are worthy.
You are strong.

How our judges and readers responded...

What a moving, empowering poem. ♥ *I really like how your use of repetition evolves from images of destruction and pessimism to images of hope and optimism.*

BIO:

Donna is a survivor of childhood trauma and domestic abuse. Continuing on her healing path, she seeks to become a voice for the silent by raising awareness of these issues through her writing and art.

Undefined
Priya Mahadevan

Don't know where to begin
Don't know what I want to say
Don't know if it's a complaint or woe
Or something to be thankful about
But every so often, a feeling of despondency grips me
Am I doing all that I was put on this earth to accomplish?
Life is good
Love surrounds me
Elates me
Extols me
There is no dire want unfulfilled
Except perhaps this one
That I should be someone,
Who is recognized in some small way
Or, let's face it, big
To make a name in any one way
That impacts more than just my family
Family is the best
I never yearn for fame over family
Never!
I want this, not just this
I want that, but never at the cost of this
So why can't this and that coexist?
Many are that fortunate that they have both
Handling each capably and well
Meeting societal expectations
Self-defined, assured
Proclaiming legitimacy
May be I have and am,
All that I can be!
Why then is there an incompletion in me?
Delightful are the moments
Not replicable
Seeing my children grow
And become stellar human beings
Thinking independently

Making life's decisions
Shaping their futures
How wonderful is the involvement
In these crucial moments
Love rules
Love dictates
Love binds
At time in agony
Other times, in ecstasy
How many women
Honestly confess
That the ups and downs
The deep distress
That engulfs every now and then
Are often wrought by hormonal spikes or dips
Questioning one's worth
Trying to measure
Quantify
Playing devil's advocate
Against our better judgment
Doling out freely
The verdict of not worthy enough
Seeking that elusive
Un-gettable something
That is not you, not yours
The restlessness is claustrophobic
Emotions rack the body and mind
And then it's done
The dam bursts
Bleeding hearts
Wake up from a sleepless night
The search is over
Love surrounds again
The sounds of life as I know it
What a sweet serenade
I feel worthy again
A welcome reprieve before
Hopelessness grips
Tumultuous and covert,
Greening the patch of grass

Challenge into Change

Far yonder,
A fingertip beyond reach
To rule for another day
Or two or three
Monthly menace
Set me free!

How our judges and readers responded...

The concept of playing devil's advocate against oneself encapsulates this poem's message. ♥ *This poem traces the coexistence of gratitude and ambition, as well as the emotional turbulence that that incongruity can incite.* ♥ *This poem is compelling: I can feel the tension the speaker expresses!*

BIO:

Mom. Chef. Writer. Entrepreneur. These are just some of the titles you could give Priya Mahadevan. Priya, a mother of three, lives in Central Virginia. She was a political journalist before she started cooking professionally, and her gift for writing is one she has kept up over the years. She recently published a bi-cultural children's picture book called Princesses Only Wear Putta Puttas. In her free time she writes poetry and has 4 other manuscripts for picture books ready with the second one being illustrated. She also teaches cooking classes around Charlottesville and does many food gigs around town. She is a strong advocate of vegetarianism.

Greedy for an Education
Michelle McSherrey

1973 – 1975
I moved to Arizona with my family in 1973. I attended Lake Havasa High School in Lake Havasa City, Arizona. These were good years, looking back on them. I learned composition and Grammatical English, as well as History, Government, Free Enterprise, Southwest History (took a few field trips to interesting places) and Psychology. Fun times.

The night I picked up my diploma (June 6th, 1975) something inside of me said "This isn't enough, I want a college education."

1976 – 1980
My first experience away from parental control. I had hopes and dreams of starting a new life: College.

I chose Northern Arizona University in Flagstaff, Arizona because it was a small university. I could even go out to bars and drink and discos to dance and country western bars to drink and cowboy dance.

My first semester was hard, and I tried to adjust to college life but I was overloaded with too many hard classes at once. And some of my dorm mates thought I was mentally retarded and should be in the military. Plus, I started to drink heavily. At first I thought drinking was glamorous but few years later it would turn ugly.

My first semester, my grades were so low that I received Academic Probation. What was I going to do?

Here's what:
Second semester I started to study, do homework, and write term papers in the library on campus. I took a smaller class load than the semester before but I continued to drink when I wasn't studying or going to classes.

Challenge into Change

My grades improved and I was in good standing on my spring semester in 1977 report card.

I never knew I had Asperger's then. I just tried to take whatever college life dealt me. I was a Health Science major but throughout I would also take electives and Liberal Studies courses.

Also in 1978 – my drinking habits turned ugly on me (I almost got a drunk in public in August 1978 that sobered me up for 3 weeks until fall semester 1978 – start of my junior year.)

At the end of spring semester 1979, I don't know how I did it, but I made academic honors, Dean's List. I say that because I was a full blown alcoholic at the time. It was God's grace that got me through my years in college. I graduated from NAU in May 1980 at the Sky Dome.

1981 – 1982

During the summer of 1980, I floundered around Tucson, Arizona. Got into mental health counseling, drinking, listening to K.CVG Radio in Tucson. More drinking and watching "Hee Haw" on Saturdays.

After a summer of no structure, I applied for Graduate School at the University of Arizona with a Major in Health Education. I started in Spring semester (January 1981) with Health Education related classes and finished in December 1982 with Education related classes. Still more drinking and now OD-ing on Tab Kola and Caffeine pills.

Well I passed my Comps. I did not have to write a thesis for my program. I finished with a "B" average and I graduated on December 15th 1982 with a Masters of Education.

Afterword

It took a while to get decent work and longer to sober up.

In 1985, after a series of underpaid odd jobs, I obtained a decent job in Santa Cruz County, Arizona and lasted for 5 years.

In the early 1990's, I came out as a female (transgender female). I moved to Virginia on September 12, 1994. Today I am sober and committed to my sobriety. I do volunteer work when I can and also, I am church going woman.

God's grace was with me for all of these years.

How our judges and readers responded...

What an impactful account of a lifetime of struggles faced and overcome. ♥ *You write with a clear eye about your addiction, but equally clear is your admirable ambition and love of learning.* ♥ *Thank you for sharing your journey toward a sober life and a life of learning—it will be an inspiration to others.*

Twice Delivered

Jeanette Meade

I was not quite three when my mother gave birth to my brother in a rudimentary Blue Ridge Mountain cabin. Fourteen days later, she walked two miles down that mountain and handed him through the window of a car to complete strangers. With nary a word, he was whisked away, never to be seen or heard from again.

I was ultimately raised with two much younger sisters in a Madison County hollow without running water or electricity, by an abusive, bootlegging Grenddeddy and under the protective wing of our Granny. We had been left there by our mother after I was repeatedly sexually abused by my step-father. Because of our age difference, I was never close to my younger sisters, leaving me forlorn much of the time. With little self-esteem and no sense of purpose until at the age of twelve, a classmate told me that I had a brother out there. After receiving confirmation from Granny and without so much as a name to aid me, I began my needle-in-a-haystack search for my younger half-brother.

Years later, while reading my palm, a psychic observed that I had a brother; yet I didn't have a brother. Asking if that made sense, only managing a nod, tears began to well up in my eyes as she proceeded to tell me that my half-brother could be found in one of the C-states.

Five decades after that fateful day on Berry Mountain, a personalized Christmas card was discovered in a neighbor's attic containing a photograph of a baby and the names I needed to aid me in my search. Against my husband's wishes, I hired a second private investigator early in 2008. On Christmas day, he informed me that he had found him.

A well-kept family secret, my brother grew up in the San Francisco Bay Area, in a "C-state," an only child, never knowing that he was not the natural son of the parents who raised him. However lonely his upbringing was, he never yearned for anything except for siblings. Fortuitously, his parents had always told him that he was born in a car out in the Virginia countryside. It was during our initial phone conversation that my jarringly familiar version of how he was born got his attention.

A subsequent DNA test revealed that we are actually full siblings. We've since become very close. Further conversations revealed that we both had many things in common. As incredible as it may sound, my first daughter and his wife share the same first and middle names. Despite what his birth certificate says, he now knows that he was actually born in Madison, not Albemarle County. He's also learned that there was an Aunt Paige in his biological lineage. Years prior to that revelation, his first granddaughter, Madison Paige was born. Too many to mention, these implausible parallels are but a few of what some might call countless coincidences or perhaps divine intervention.

How our judges and readers responded…

This is a story of great bravery and rewarding persistence! ♥ *The author's story of reunion is both heartbreaking and inspiring. It represents the uncanniness of biological relations and sibling interests.*

BIO:

I'm a retired great grandmother who currently resides in Ruckersville, Virginia. I grew up in a Madison hollow without running water or electricity, in the care of my grandparents with two of my four sisters during the 1950s and 1960s.

Challenge into Change

FULL CIRCLE
Allyson Mescher

People ask me all the time where I'm from. I honestly don't know how to respond to that question. I was born in Illinois, moved to South Carolina as a teenager, lived in Colorado as a married mother of 3, and finally landed in Virginia as a divorced mother of 3. You'd think this would make me a well-rounded person. But, in reality, all I was doing was following other people… first parents, a husband, then friends. "Round and round Allyson goes. But where she stops, nobody knows."

As a child, I always dreamed about the day I would get married and have children. Even though I had the opportunity to go to college and have a "career," I wanted a traditional life. You know, the white-picket fence, house in suburbia, dog named Spot, the whole 9 yards!! My mom was a stay-at-home mom and raised my two brothers and me. She was a Superwoman and could do anything!! I wanted to be just like her and hoped for the same kind of life one day.

I thought I had achieved my dream when I met my ex-husband. He was in the Navy, charming, and whisked me off my feet. However, my dream soon crumbled before my eyes shortly after we married. He was physically, emotionally, and verbally abusive. He was also controlling and manipulative, so no one believed me about the abuse. I became like a shell, hollow and empty on the inside. I put up with his crap for 13 long years. However, the final straw came when I found out he abused our 3 children in the worst way possible!! It took every ounce of strength I had, but I was a mama bear protecting her cubs!! My children and I eventually got justice!!

Today, I have been divorced for 15 years and will be turning 50 years old this year. Ironically, I am asking myself the same question I did so many years ago: "How am I going to do it?" My children are grown and I am officially an "empty-nester." I am scared of an uncertain future just like I was back then.

The Women's Initiative is helping me with issues from my past and with the "empty-nest syndrome." My daughter recently told me: "I'm alive and I'm here." Guess I really have come full-circle.

How our judges and readers responded...

You really clearly express the journey you've been through. ♥ *It's so inspiring to see how your positivity endured despite the obstacles you've faced.*

Anxiety
Patricia W. Pollock

Around and around the circular room I went, tears gushing down my face, scraping my elbows and knees on the hard concrete surface of the room's walls. How had I suddenly gone into this madness, when months ago I had been in my comfortable home, which would be mine no more, and my job of teaching special education classes to which I wanted to devote the rest of my life? It was all because of this terrible illness that had overtaken me. Because of the terrible depressions that would make it hard for me to work, and the crippling anxiety that would keep me unable to be still, and my desire to get along with my life, that had brought me here. This place, NIMH, was supposed to have the answers, but was the price too high?

It was not my wish to be here, but my doctor's idea. I think she had run out of ideas for my treatment, and tired of my case, and I had allowed myself to get so dependent on her that I never considered getting another doctor for fear of being rejected. So I had signed up for six months of treatment in this experimental protocol.

So this seemed to be my last chance at sanity, and I was scared of being forced to leave without a cure. I was taken off all of the medication that had imperfectly kept me together and given another medication that was all an experiment.

My anxiety level increased instead of leveling out, and I suffered from delusions that thus was not a safe place and the doctors were trying to hurt me with those little pink research pills. Soon I feared staying in my own room, because I had visions of knocking over furniture, or hurting someone. That is how I ended up in the seclusion room, a round room with a hard floor and concrete walls, because I didn't trust myself to be around people. When I explained to the doctor how I was hurting myself, his only reply was that if I broke a leg or something, they would send me home. Those dreaded words, to go home without a cure.

Eventually the experiment came to an end, without a cure for me. Instead of going home, I went to another hospital since I was at risk of ending my life. It took three months for me to find myself again, and when I left the hospital I still suffered from recurrent depressions.

About five years later, I was put on Prozac, and I found at least part of my cure. The rest of the cure came not in a pill, but in action. I had started a support group called Even Keel which I still run today for people suffering from mental health problems. Also about four years ago I joined On Our Own, a peer recovery center, where I volunteer to help other with mental challenges like mine. With a sense of purpose and medication, I lead a very happy and satisfying life. My purpose in life is to spread the word that there is recovery from mental illness, and to help people like me do it.

How our judges and readers responded...

It's so brave of you to share this harrowing, deeply personal story. ♥ *The rich details you write of your struggles with anxiety are heartrending, but I'm glad to hear that you've gotten better, and are now sharing your narrative to offer hope for others.*

BIO:

Patricia Pollock was born in 1949 in Amityville, New York. She grew up in Charlottesville, Virginia and graduated from Lane High School, and later from Virginia Tech with a BS in Biology. She attended the University of Virginia to get her teaching credentials to teach special education. In 1976, she started suffering from recurrent depressions. At the present time she is a volunteer and board member for On Our Own, a peer recovery center located in Charlottesville, VA. She is also a volunteer at UVA hospital where she runs a peer support group on the psychiatric unit.

Standing for the Silent
Jojo Robertson

The most horrible tragedy that ever struck my family was at a church. The church was our way of life. However, the one place that we called home, that we spent all of our time at, the same place that we found refuge at suddenly became a place we feared.

My child almost died at the church. One evening, the children's minister allowed her children who were a little bit older to watch the younger children. Her children had a really rough life. Their father was an alcoholic, the parents were going through a really nasty divorce. Only two weeks before her son busted almost killed my child the father of the boy had the kids for the weekend. In a drunken rage he beat down some doors and destroyed some items in their house.

The children's pastor left all of the children alone to have an argument with her teenage daughter outside of the gym. She had instructed her kids to watch the kids in the gym. My son had a little spiderman toy and was playing with it. The children minister came up to him and told my son he wanted it. My son who was 5 said no this boy who was 10. The boy with a blue belt in kicked my son over and over.

The next thing that occurred was the children's minister bringing my son to me. She said he had fallen but got straight up. My son looked reddish and flushed. I made the decision to take him to the hospital. My son had a ruptured spleen, broken ribs and bowel contusions. I remember his screams cries as if it was yesterday.

The Pastor of the church came up to the hospital. He said that the truth may cause people not to believe in God and make them go to hell. He said that if people lost their salvation, it would be our fault. He told my son that if he told about what happened he would have no friends growing up. I should have spat at him and told him to leave. Instead I sat in fear. At that time I was a meek girl who was scared of authority. All authority scared me.

One may think that my faith is God was shaken, and it was, but my relationship with him became stronger. I realized that no man should come between my faith, and I realized that the Pastor was a wolf in sheep's' clothing. I realized that God was my strength, not man. God knows what that Pastor did, and God is in charge. Even though there are people in his congregation that know exactly what happened that night they still go to that church. They are simply cowards. Although man's legal laws may not affect the Pastor and his congregation, (they were able to claim charitable immunity), and maybe he does have a lot of power in this community, but there is one thing he cannot control, and that is my story. My word, my experience and my passion are three things he will never have control of.

I started an anti-bullying chapter called Stand for the Silent in Albemarle. Stand for the Silent is an non-profit anti-bullying group that our family has been a part of for 6 years. I go where ever is needed and teach kids about their rights. And how to stand up to bullies and seek out help.

Where does this leave me now? It allows me to help others that may be experiencing the pains of bullying. It allows me to switch from being a victim, to becoming a warrior. I personally have been through so much, but I can either allow it to either break me or make me. For me I choose the later.

Challenge into Change

How our judges and readers responded…

This is such a captivating and immersive story that I did not want it to end. So many lines draw me into the story and made me feel like I was there with the author: "I remember his screams cries as if it was yesterday" and "I should have spat at him and told him to leave." ♥ Every line really tells us the emotion of the events and the journey that the author had to take to end up in the incredible position of a warrior for those who are silent and powerless around her. ♥ What an inspiring and powerful human being!

BIO:

Jojo Robertson can be found in schools, churches, businesses and anywhere that would like to learn how to become Upstanders and fight the devastating effects of bullying. Jojo has two amazing kids that she considers gifts from God. In her spare time, she likes to read, talk, and be a positive force in her community.

I Am, That I Am
Mary Rodwell

As children we grow up not fully knowing the Pros and Cons of decisions we've made. I guess some would say it's all a part of life. Growing up in a high-crime area wasn't so easy for one young girl named Tutu. She lived behind a fenced in two bedroom house with her parents and four siblings. Tutu had great hope for her family, but things changed once she received some heartbreaking news. As a result, she found herself over the years stepping outside that fence. Tutu was stuck between two ways of living "Hot Pursuit" versus "High Pursuit". Based on a true story, about Mary Rodwell. You will learn how she went from being rebellious to righteous. This story will make you cry, laugh and learn at the same time.

Was born to Arthur & Gladys Rodwell, raised in Richmond, Virginia; she is the fifth of seven children. After the passing of her father Mary was left broken and in great despair looking for someone else to mend her heart. From being a teenager to her adulthood she struggled to find her purpose in life and love. Although Mary experienced some trials and tribulations in life; she didn't let it get the best of her. Being a strong woman, Mary took a stand and made the most out of every situation! At a very early age she was introduced to God & accepted the Father as her Lord and Savior. This act of courage allowed Mary to know and feel love.

How our judges and readers responded...

This story suggests great pain, but it also manifests self-assurance and tenacity.
♥ The image of a woman torn between two versions of herself is both engaging and relatable.

BIO:

Mary is a single mother of two, bestselling author, 1 of 6 top contestants for the 2016 NAACP Image Hometown Champion Award for her hometown, RPS 2015-2016 Elkhardt Thompson Middle School Title 1 Outstanding Parent, writer, anti-bully representative and dynamic motivational speaker. She's gifted by God to motivate and preach the good news.

Remembering Irene
Michele J. Rolle

Compassionate, professional and caring- Mammography Technologist are not just made we are created. This is how I was created.

The puddle of urine in the floor should have been an indicator of how hard and painful, my fumbled positioning and compression of her breast on this rigid platform affected her.

I should have recognized this adult woman before me was incapable of verbally communicating her pain. But I was a young, inexperienced and insensitive mammography technologist. Her non-verbal clues went unnoticed, until I literally stepped into the puddle of urine at my feet.

I provided her with hospital scrubs to change into and washed her soiled clothes in my sink. Bundling them tightly for her bus ride home, I imagined the smell of urine on her ride home would have exacerbated her shame and humiliation. I later learned she lived in a facility for functional and intellectually disabled adults.

Earlier in my career as a radiologic technologist, I performed what is often described as routine x-rays, i.e., chest x-rays, etc.

Most of the "routine exams" required little emotional contact with patient. The patients were in and out, and I would move on to the next one. This was mundane and robotic.

Then a radiologic technologist entered my life, for a season.

We worked weekends together, and she demonstrated the purest example of professionalism and compassionate care to every patient she encountered.

Challenge into Change

171

I did not know until her final days on this side of heaven, that she wore a wig to cover her baldness and that her spontaneous trips to the bathroom were the result of side effects from the Chemotherapy.

What I did know was that she was an incredible wife and mother to her long awaited new born baby.

She never accepted special treatment or sympathy during her battle against breast cancer: she was an "Invisible Warrior".

I still recall the last time I saw her lying in the hospital bed. Her spirit was strong, her countenance so beautiful and as her breathing became more laborious, I knew her time to make her transition was rapidly approaching.

I told her how much I loved her, and I felt glued in the space where I stood. Her mother sensing my hesitancy to leave, gave me permission, in a soft, quiet tone, she simply said, "Its OK, you can leave".

I kissed her softly on her cheek and with her head already turned toward the window, I left the room.

When the elevator reached the lobby floor, for a minute I wanted to press her floor and return to see her one last time. I didn't, instead I sat in my car and wept.

I had never left someone knowing it would be the last time I would ever see them again. She made her transition that evening, leaving behind her husband and new born daughter.

She also left an example for me to use as a blueprint for the beginning of what I knew would be a Healthcare journey of making an effective difference with my patients, by demonstrating what compassionate care feels and looks like.

How our judges and readers responded...

This essay weaves together the stories of three women to demonstrate the emotional labor of patient care. ♥ *I appreciate that you represent these women as having both emotional and physical needs.*

BIO:

Michele J. Rolle is a Mammography healthcare specialist in Richmond, Virginia, and has been compassionately committed for more than 25 years to educating and mentoring women in the value of breast health. Michele works for a prominent Obstetrics and Gynecology practice and has represented them as a Chief Mammography Technologist in her appearances on television, radio, and newspaper, and has been quoted in many publications. Michele is the Author of her debut memoir "Invisible Warrior".

Challenge into Change

Explosive Material Is Best Treated with Prayer!
Amelia Rose

At the height of the Fall Season, the porches and entryways were decorated for the holiday. The evenings and weekends were the best opportunity for our family to enjoy time together. Like, quiet evenings around the fire pit looking at the stars and roasting marshmallows. Our family game nights often included cookouts. We seemed like we were the perfect couple to many. Most of the time ours was a happy home, except for the days when this reliable man suddenly erupted without considering the consequences. It was his downfall, he became agitated by unimportant things. This caused a lot of marital tension since it left me with the fallout from his explosion. I quickly left the room, then closed the wooden door to a spare room and switched on the television. It was my only escape from my hostile husband. I needed the distraction of the TV to calm my nerves after the onslaught of his contempt. I couldn't say the things I wanted to say, knowing it wouldn't have made a difference. I learned to walk softly around him in times of his arsenal attacks. Even though I managed to walk away, the residual effects of his venomous bites tore at my heart. Only pain remained with my tears.

I knelt down by the side of the bed and emptied the emotional pain into my prayers. Maybe it was going to take some time for the wounds to heal. The first few minutes were the most difficult to sift through. But, as I lay my burdens before the Lord, His love restored my soul. At the same time, I believe that the Holy Spirit went to work on my husband's heart. I suddenly realized that our children would soon be home from school and we hadn't even spoken a word.

I went to the kitchen to begin the prep for our evening meal. I was doing my best to avoid him, as he stood behind me and offered to help. "What's the matter?" He asked. I slowly opened a cabinet door for another spice to add into the marinade. I am not a professional counselor, but I think that he was hoping that this would be an acceptable time for him to apologize. I handed him a large tomato and asked him to dice it. The awkwardness passed; It seems that we have our best discussions when we engage in an activity. Fortunately, we moved forward and didn't drag the children into an atmosphere of hard feelings.

During these times your faith, and the power of prayer are exercised. I didn't invite marital tension or heartache, in fact, I would prefer to live without them. I am convinced beyond a shadow of doubt that when the irrational behavior begins I need to treat it like the poison it is.

Beware! Don't drink the poison. Remove yourself from the dumping ground because explosive material is best treated with PRAYER!

How our judges and readers responded...

"It's really lovely how you interweave your history with your husband with a specific portrait of the two of you at home on one evening. ♥ The description of the two of you cooking, and talking better when your hands are busy, is very moving; it rings true."

BIO:

Amelia Rose has been practicing the art of writing for the past four years. She has entered a few of her writings for consideration. In addition, she is a member of ACFW and Toastmasters. She has received a certificate for Business. Her notable achievements have been involved with raising a family of two fine boys and a beautiful girl. Currently she is working on her first fictional novel, and she resides in the Tri-City Area of Virginia.

Challenge into Change

Dutch Tulips
Dylan Roth

"I need to talk to you. Can you sit down?"

Those aren't the words that you want to hear when you're eleven. But they're the words that you remember. The normal words of everyday disappear from your memories and the only words that remain are "I have to go back to the hospital again, it'll be ok this time." Those are the words I remember.

I remember my mother being gone for days and sometimes weeks. With less of her coming back home each time. I remember when we had to buy a fold out bed for the living room because she had to get up so much during the night. And that time she let me cut her hair when I was twelve since it was going to fall out anyway. I remember staying awake at night, waiting for her to stop crying or sometimes screaming. I waited for her to fall asleep before I would lay down. I remember her view from Beth Israel of Fenway off in the distance. And that dreadful clean smell of her room. The charts, the tubes, the medicine. The doctors saying that with bone marrow cancer you only have two shots at beating it with a transfusion. I remember that longed-for second remission, and the stroke that soon followed. I remember teaching her to read again and how sad she looked when she couldn't remember a word. All those bad things. I remember sitting in my bedroom alone knowing she was never coming home again.

But I remember a woman who never stopped going to work until they made her. And then she worked at home, setting up the computer in my bedroom so we could hang out. She came to my volleyball games, my band concerts, my dance recitals and my teacher conferences. She drove me and my friends to school every day that she could. She packed my lunch before I even woke up. She still wore her makeup every day and even let me convince her to buy a blonde wig once. When she was in the hospital, she would still call to make

176   *Challenge into Change*

sure that I did my homework. She watched movies with me every weekend and read the same books so we could talk about them. She put Christmas presents on layaway, so we could still have something and pay medical bills. She rested up for days so we could go pick out my prom dress together. When she couldn't remember how to say words, but still said my name. She did everything I could ever need, until she couldn't.

I remember a woman who wouldn't be told "no" because she had cancer. You couldn't tell her to stop. I remember a woman who refused to let dying become her life. She didn't want her dying to become my life. She did everything she could to make things as they should have been. To keep going. To keep me going. Everything.

So now, I just remember her.

How our judges and readers responded...

An extremely powerful piece. Rich, compelling. Moving portrait of a courageous mother. ♥ *The author showed us in her writing that she had two roles as a child—that of being a daughter and sometimes role of the mother in that she was helping her mother do things a mother would normally do for her child. When she could've been distant because of all the adulting she had to do as a child, she chose not to be. She was there for her mother.* ♥ *What an amazing tribute to the determination and loving spirit of a mother who will not give up no matter her circumstances.* ♥ *The writing lifts the reader up and reminds us that life is not about the where we go but how far we have traveled to get there.*

BIO:

I'm originally from the great white north. I studied literature at Emerson College (BA) and the University of Denver (MLS). I am also an Air Force veteran. Writing and books have always been in my life because of my mother, who passed away when I was 17. She loved black eyeliner, coffee and elephants. And so do I.

Challenge into Change

Youthful Grievances

Kieran Rundle

I made a list of the things I could apologize for
and it was as long as the sum
of seconds that it took for your lips to part
and words to form on the tip of your
tongue burnt from too hot coffee,
after our gaze
shattered.

It filled the corners of your eyes and
rolled down your cheeks
in a distraught mechanical rhythm
that tear drops
could only dream
of perfecting,
and rain was too terrified
to break.

My sarcasm and wit
did not lighten the mood,
but seemed to dim the lights
for which we could not even pay.
The 94 cent
warm apple pie
candle-
from the super walmart down the street-
flickered
and went out.

Odd, isn't it, how a homey scent
can make you feel
even more isolated
from yourself?

My list stretched out in the form
of a silently extended hand
and I gently lowered
my guilt onto the scale
of honesty
in front of us,
in hopes that you would see it.
Instead-
you saw through it
to the way my fishnet stockings
formed rings on my skin;
my crop top
was one lie too short
for your liking.

My makeup was muddy
and the bruises
forming on my skin
had fingerprints.
You had no need for a magnifying glass,
or to relight the candle,
to identify the perpetrator.

So you sipped your coffee,
cold now,
and closed your eyes.
You deemed my matters
a trivial "I told you so".

"Your eyes look like
sex and marijuana,"
you commented on my rouged complexion,
not needed to look at me
in order to assess
the situation
and to place the odor of

Challenge into Change   179

overpowering incense
that my skirt exhumed.

I could have explained,
presented a powerpoint
on how I made the
right choice
tonight
and why my eye
was black
and my lips
were crusted
in dried blood
that flaked off like the remains
of your trust.

Instead,
my three inch heels clicked
up the wood stairs,
and my list of apologies
stretched like a kite string.
You tethered me to the ground,
and with each nuclear gust higher
the tension
increased.
As my door locked
shut-
the string snapped
and you set your coffee
down on the table,
cold now.

How our judges and readers responded...

The way this narrative poem uses words to tell the story of an emotionally charged interaction takes the reader on a journey with the characters and creates a deep understanding of how regret can simmer until it boils over as a catalyst for action. ♥ *Passionate and angry tone—distinct, unconventional voice.*

BIO:

Kieran Rundle, a high school student, is the owner and editor-in-chief for Sincerely Magazine LLC. She is on staff for Miracle Magazine, and has worked for four years as an upper editor on Albemarle High School's Literary Magazine. She is an award-winning artist, poet, prose writer, and playwright. Her work can be found in a plethora of places including Charlottesville Area Transit Busses, The UVA Special Collections Library, Quail Bell Magazine, and the Crossroads III Anthology. She is also an avid theatre dweller, cat lover, stargazer, cookie eater, and chocolate addict.

Finding What's Eating Me
Sera S.

I am 9 years old, sitting in Dad's Subaru, shoving fries into my mouth. If Mom were here this food would not be approved, and this conversation would be a fight. I eat more than I should, faster than I should, way past full. I have so much more to worry about than full and besides, I like how my mind wanders away from what he is saying as I eat.

"If I lived in your house," Dad reminds my sister and me, "you wouldn't get away with not listening. Your Mom just doesn't know what she is doing." I focus on the salt on the fries, which feels so much better than this conversation. I can't say anything to Dad. Any response would leave me hurting one of the two people I love and rely on for my most basic needs.

I stay quiet and eat.

Eating was a good solution, until junior high, when I learned that if I wanted to be an accepted and loved girl, I needed to be thin. I wasn't heavy at a size 7, but the reflection I saw in the mirror didn't tell me that. I needed to be smaller. I skipped breakfast, ate 4 crackers and skim milk for lunch, went to 2-3 hours of sports practice. Mom cooked dinner and, ravenous, I would eat all she made and much more. Mortified, I would go into the bathroom, lock the door, and purge.

Mom caught me.

I couldn't stop.

Mom found me a therapist. I reminded her I did not have a problem, but I liked the time with her in the car to and from appointments, so I went for several months.

In college, my binges soaked up my hangovers. My purges stopped. I gained weight and hated myself. I was in a fog, so I kept eating and drinking. It was the only time I felt okay.

When I got my first corporate job, I knew I needed a new solution. I began to workout multiple times a day. Half marathon training and races became my purge of choice. I got to a size 4. I had reached my goal, but I had not found happiness or acceptance. I was still me.

Finally, I searched for help on my own. I learned that my eating disorder was not about my body. It was about shame that lived deep inside me, from my childhood and my own past dysfunctional relationships with men. That shame had kept me a prisoner in my own body. When I found a group of safe people that allowed me to share my truth, while still loving and accepting me, I healed.

I could see that the more I tried to control, the more out of control my body and life became. Once I began to share my story and let God guide my path, I could finally live in my life, as it was, and have happiness, acceptance and peace, no matter my size.

How our judges and readers responded…

Overcoming an eating disorder is so difficult. You describe this terrible problem with clarity and insight. Strong and spare. Clear, concise writing. ♥ This well-written piece leads the reader to a deeper understanding of the challenges that lead one to seek escape through the illusion of control. ♥ The well-built and carefully chosen sentences allow the writer's voice to guide the reader through a life-journey that culminates in self-acceptance and openness to the future.

Challenge into Change

BIO:

Sera is on a mission to use her voice, experience and passion for wellness to inspire healthy change. As a cancer survivor and woman in recovery from an eating disorder, Sera uses her life's story to challenge the way we honor our personal health and overall wellness. She is an advocate of a holistic approach to health and shares openly about how combining traditional and complementary therapies helps her thrive.

Follow Your Dreams?

Sharon Showalter

This is a story about learning how to dream. Doesn't everyone dream? Don't children dream about their lives, hopes, and desires? Does one ever stop dreaming?

Before we move to dreams, I will share my story, which is really not that unusual, unfortunately. I was born 57 years ago. My parents had their own struggles before I arrived. My mother lived a life of hard work, poverty, and too little love. My father's life was similar, yet his was made more challenging by World War II and the horrors of battle. Sadly, no one knew about PTSD in those days. My father coped by becoming an alcoholic; my mother coped by working hard. I am one of three daughters.

Our life was filled with terror, violence, abuse, little food-not enough. My father was what many call a 'mean' alcoholic, but I suspect the 'happy' alcoholics wreak havoc in their own way. I won't cause you discomfort by sharing too many sad stories; I will provide a glimpse so that you understand my path. I recall a time when I was about six years old; my drunken father went to the kitchen cupboard and retrieved a knife, screaming at my mother that he would "cut her heart out and eat it". Imagine the fear. Similar stories are far too abundant.

Through years of therapy, coping in my own unhealthy ways, and eventually coming to a place of recovery, I was startled by the realization that I never had dreams. This discovery caused immense sadness. I was so focused on mere survival – living moment to moment, not knowing what the next would bring – I never dreamed. There were no dreams of getting married one day, having children, owning a home, having enough. There were no dreams of Santa's gifts or dreams of a new coat as I flipped through the JC Penny catalog. I had NO dreams. I lived my life as I had learned – work hard, save money, don't let anyone 'see' me, don't talk about the past (no one can know!) -just make it through.

Challenge into Change

I began noticing things-greeting cards about 'hope your dreams come true'; small gift items bearing the words 'follow your dreams'; others talking about their dreams 'coming true', and seeing 'Living the Dream' everywhere. How did I miss out on all of this? I had never learned to dream.

After enduring anger and sadness most of my life (and after reclaiming faith), I made a conscious decision to forgive my parents. Yes, it's possible. They were ill. They did the best they could. I discovered this as I found myself ill; I understood. I was free.

Soon, I began to dream. I became a nurse. I love my tiny little home. I love my dogs. I practice random acts of kindness. I notice little things (a bee on a flower) and feel gratitude. These are MY dreams. I don't 'dream big' as I am blessed and finally have 'enough'.

How our judges and readers responded…

Thank you for sharing this heart-wrenching and extremely personal story—that took a lot of courage. ♥ *I really like the way you move from the overarching narrative—the shape of your early life—to specific anecdotes, like the moments of fear you experience with your father. Later in the narrative, you do a beautiful job of showing, again through anecdote, how you came to realize that you had the right to your own dreams.*

BIO:

I live in Charlottesville. My life had (yes, past tense) been a life of struggle and sadness. Despite formidable life circumstances, I worked hard, received a full scholarship and became a Nurse. I have nursed in trauma, oncology, and hospice (currently). I hope I have made a difference. I live simply. I finally feel free to be myself. I find pleasure in small things. I practice acts of kindness. I feel gratitude. My life is abundant. I have dreams.

Ms. Maitreya, a Haiku
Slavin

Being that is me -
needy, greedy, hard, hope-fool -
places foot on Path

How our judges and readers responded...

The play on words with "hope-fool" is so striking and made me both nervous and excited for the woman's journey. ♥ *Even though this poem is short, I feel like I know the woman it describes.*

BIO:

As a dirt-poor coal-miner's daughter's daughter. my choice to escape the effects of an abusive mother and dysfunctional family was simple: fall into the abyss or take the hand offered to be pulled out. They say when you are ready a teacher will appear. Buddhism says that when we are experiencing pain and strife we are burning away impure karma from the past. I believe both.

Escribiendo mi Historia, el Diario de una Mexicana

Coco Sotelo

Aquí empieza mi historia de cuando llegue a este país. Mi vida dio un giro de 360 grados, estaba aquí, en una tierra lejana del país y el lugar que me vio nacer, Arcelia Guerrero México. Frente a mí había un mundo desconocido con un millón de retos por enfrentar esperando a que me decidiera y comenzara a caminar hacia adelante.

¿Fue difícil? Definitivamente SÍ. Primero que nada, encontré la barrera de la lengua, no hablaba inglés y por la tanto no podía comunicarme. Eso fue realmente fuerte para mí puesto que soy una mujer que por naturaleza me encanta conversar, socializar, hacer amigos y por profesión soy Comunicóloga (Periodista) en mi país, es decir siempre he hecho uso de la palabra en todo momento y bum! de la noche a la mañana me convertí prácticamente muda. El silencio, la frustración y la tristeza vinieron a mi vida. Fue un cambio para el que no estaba preparada.

Al mismo tiempo mi familia y yo atravesamos la etapa de la adaptación cultural, ¿cómo encajar en una cultura desconocida? Las circunstancias, las buenas personas que se cruzaron en nuestros caminos en ese momento y la vida misma nos fue enseñando no solo a vivir, si no a aprender la cultura anglosajona y a mantener lo mejor de nuestra cultura mexicana para poder transmitirla a nuestras hijas.

Mis primeros años en Charlottesville fueron muy difíciles, me encontré realmente sola, a pesar de que la familia de mi esposo vive aquí, debido a la diferencia de nivel intelectual, valores, maneras distintas de vivir y de ver la vida jamás fui bien recibida en la familia por lo tanto vinieron muchísimos problemas familiares que terminaron en una fuerte depresión y ganas de separarme de mi esposo para no tener una cercanía con su familia. En este momento crucial de nuestras vidas Dios nos habló al corazón y decidimos acercarnos a ÉL, tomamos terapia de pareja y decidimos luchar por nuestra familia. Con la ayuda de la terapista mi esposo logró identificar y cortar los patrones de vida y de familia que no nos gustaban y juntos decidimos luchar y caminar del otro lado del camino para buscar la felicidad.

Después de muchas caídas y levantadas alzamos el vuelo y aquí estamos a través de la constancia, trabajo duro, dedicación y paciencia logramos establecer nuestro pequeño negocio de limpieza el cual nos ha dado la oportunidad de conocer gente realmente maravillosa que se han convertido en familia, la oportunidad de dedicarle tiempo a nuestras hijas y la oportunidad de servir a los demás.

En el 2016 fundé otro negocio junto a mis dos hijas mayores "Gaona Granola Co." Producimos granolas artesanales, las empaquetamos y las vendemos.

Gaona Granola me dio la oportunidad de estudiar un certificado en negocios y mostrarme a la comunidad como una empresaria mexicana.

Y en este momento simplemente contando nuestras bendiciones.......

Reza, Ama, Vive y Sueña

Challenge into Change

Cómo respondieron nuestros jueces y lectores…

¡Qué historia tan inspiradora! Hay tantas adversidades en un país nuevo, y además tuviste que lidiar con tantos problemas personales. ¡Pero tú los venciste! Felicitaciones. ♥ Quedo impresionada con la autora, una persona de coraje, fuerza, y sinceridad. Admirable atención por mejorar su situación en América. Claro compromiso con sus valores, voluntad de trabajar muy duro. ♥ Creo que esta mujer -y sus hijas- van a triunfar. ♥ La autora es una prueba más que cuando no tienes otra opción más que tener éxito en un ambiente desafiante, haremos lo necesario para hacer precisamente eso. Como resultado, esta autora no fundó uno sino dos empresas. La inmigración puede arrancar gente de todo lo que conocen y colocarlo en un mundo nuevo y aterrador, lleno de inseguridad. Con prosa conmovedora, esta historia sigue ese camino en todo su horror, pero va más allá para mostrar la trascendencia positiva que es posible con fe y dedicación.

Biografía:

Soy Periodista y Emprendedora. Soy alumna de la vida, la vida que enseña tanto! Llegue a US en el 2005, a través del tiempo me sumergí el mundo de los emprendedores. En el 2013 comencé formalmente mi pequeño negocio de limpieza y en 2016 funde Gaona Granola Co. Actualmente compagino los dos negocios como fundadora y dueña de Goana Granola Co. he completado el Entrepreneurship Workshop de CIC y seré parte del programa Accelerator 2017 de I.Lab en Darden School.

Writing My Story, the Diary of a Mexican Woman

(English translation from Spanish)

Coco Sotelo

Here begins my story of when I arrive in this country. My life took a 360-degree turn, I was here in a land far away from the country and the place where I was born, Arcelia Guerrero Mexico. In front of me was an unknown world with a million challenges to face waiting for me to make decisions and begin to move forward.

Was it difficult? Definitely YES. First of all, I found the language barrier, I did not speak English, so I could not communicate and that was really hard for me since I am a woman who by nature loves to talk, socialize, make friends and by profession I am a communicator (journalist) in my country. That is to say I have always made use of the word at all times, and boom! overnight I became practically mute. Silence, frustration and sadness came into my life. It was a change I was not ready for.

At the same time, my family and I were going through the stage of cultural adaptation, how do we fit into an unknown culture? The circumstances, the good people who crossed our paths at that moment, and life itself taught us not only to live, but to learn the Anglo culture and to maintain the best of our Mexican culture in order to transmit it to our daughters.

My first years in Charlottesville were very difficult. I found myself really alone, despite the fact that my husband's family lives here, because of the difference in intellectual level, values, different ways of living and seeing life, I was never welcomed in the family; therefore, came many family problems that ended up in a strong depression and desire to separate from my husband so as not to have any closeness with his family. At this crucial moment in our lives, God spoke to our hearts and we decided to approach Him, we took couples therapy and decided to fight for our family. With the help of a therapist my husband managed to identify and cut down the patterns of life and family that we did not like and together we decided to fight and walk across the way to seek happiness.

After many ups and downs we took off and here we are through perseverance, hard work, dedication and patience we managed to establish our small cleaning business which has given us the opportunity to meet really wonderful people who have become family, the opportunity to devote time to our daughters and the opportunity to serve others.

In 2016 I founded another business together with my two older daughters "Gaona Granola Co." We produce handmade granolas, package and sell them. Gaona Granola Co. gave me the opportunity to receive a certificate in business and present myself to the community as a Mexican businesswoman.

And in this moment simply counting our blessings ....

Pray, Love, Live and Dream

How our judges and readers responded…

What an inspiring story! There are so many challenges in a new country, and you had to deal with so many personal problems as well. But you prevailed! Congratulations. ♥ *Very impressed with the writer as a person of courage, strength, and sincerity. Admirable focus on improving her situation in America. Clear commitment to her values, willingness to work very hard.* ♥ *I have the sense this woman—and her daughters—are going to succeed.* ♥ *The author is further proof that when you have no other choice but to succeed in a challenging environment, you'll do what needs to be done to do just that. As a result, this author founded not one but two businesses. Immigration can rip a people from all they know and place them in a new, terrifying world fraught with insecurity. With poignant prose, this story follows that journey in all its horror, but goes beyond to show the positive transcendence that is possible with faith and dedication.*

BIO:

I am a journalist and an entrepreneur. I am a student of life, the life that teaches me so much! I arrived in the USA in 2005, through time I immersed myself in the world of entrepreneurs. In 2013 I formally started my small cleaning business and in 2016 I founded Gaona Granola Co. I am currently managing the two businesses as founder and owner of Gaona Granola Co. I have completed the CIC Entrepreneurship Workshop and will be part of the Accelerator program 2017 of I. Lab at Darden School.

Challenge into Change

Untitled
Stormi

I'm sitting here on a mat on the bathroom floor alone. I'm crying. I've been crying for over an hour, and I don't know how to stop.

I hurt my boyfriend. A woman called my phone asking who I was. She was talking as if they were together. I told her my story trying to warn her of all he had put me through. The daily tantrums. The financial abuse. The cheating. The lying.

Instead, I learned that it was all a joke. They made me feel like a fool. Now he's mad because I put our business out there like my feelings didn't matter. He told other people too. Everyone just laughed at me. He said that I could fall for anything. Maybe he's right.

I can't seem to get anything right. I'm weak. Something is missing. I feel empty inside. Where did I go? Who am I? I can't breathe. I want to die. He told me that I would find someone else, but I don't want anyone else. I love him. He doesn't understand that. I've always wanted someone to love me, but it always falls on deaf ears. Like I'm the invisible one in a room full of people. Like I never mattered.

Maybe I should just disappear. I have problems, and I don't know how to fix them. I'm a college grad. I should be able to do anything right? I'm a journalism graduate, yet I don't know how to communicate. Isn't that ironic?

It's been nearly two hours now, and I'm still crying. The tears are flowing down my face like waterfalls. My whole body aches. My legs. My back. My head. But like the masochist that I am, I dwell in my pain. Will it ever end?

I keep telling myself, "Maybe if I just stay with him, he will pay back all of the money he stole from me as he had promised." Time and time again, I have put his needs in front of mine, thinking it would be reciprocated. When he needed money for food, I was there. When he needed money to cover court costs, I was there. I'm drowning deeper and deeper into debt. Deeper and deeper into despair. Yet, he lives as if he hasn't a care in the world.

But maybe I'm looking at it wrong. Maybe I should be proud of myself for doing what was right? I mean, I did try to protect someone else from a potentially abusive relationship.

I am an independent woman who loves hard. Loves everyone except for myself. I can't keep hurting myself. I have to learn how to love me more than I love him.

I feel like I'm finally finding myself. The tears are slowing. I can finally see again. My breathing is returning to normal.

Now, I can stand.

How our judges and readers responded…

Tears can produce self-realization and can motivate one to overcome obstacles and accept herself. ♥ *Your story channels so much pain and therefore allows the reader to identify with you and cheer you on.* ♥ *Powerful.* ♥ *You have been grappling with troubled relationships, but a resolution is near as you regain your sense of self.*

BIO:

Stormi is a talented writer with a passion for graphic design. Coming from a military family, she has lived all over the world. She graduated from Hampton University in 2008 and is currently a freelance graphic designer specializing in print design. Through her marketing efforts, she seeks to help aspiring entrepreneurs build successful businesses.

Kleenex for Lace

Maura Tierney

Being a single parent with 2 teenagers several years ago was a challenge not only physically but emotionally....We survived the chaos in relocations and loss of auto and home...what got me through the financial hardships was the courage and confidence that we would be able to find a place to live and survive together.at a low point one day I was at church and my fears and despair welled up from deep within and I started to cry silently ...I sniffled and needed to blow my nose, searching urgently through my purse, I discovered I had no Kleenex....In desperation and embarrassment ,I hesitantly turned to the woman next to me -a stranger-and asked her for a tissue... she produced a lovely white linen handkerchief ,beautifully bordered with lace.

On the way out I asked for her name and address so I could launder and return it. . .she insisted I keep it. . .a simple request became an important life lesson for me. We ask for Kleenex and He gives us lace. The healing was spiritual as well as emotional.

How our judges and readers responded...

Your story made me believe in the goodness around us. Your resilience shines through this description, showing how your own strength allowed you to be open to help from others around you. ♥ *The vivid description of the moment in the church made me feel that I was present for it; your skill as a writer really comes through there. How strongly a simple gift from another made you feel cared for and valued.* ♥ *You teach us that we should not miss opportunities to give to others. It can matter so much.*

BIO:

Maura is a retired federal employee and belongs to 2 local senior citizen groups. Maura enjoys reading, cooking, visits with family and friends, exploring new places, both nearby and out of state.

Court Square Chestnut

Sue Tiezzi

My mother is as strong and weathered as the Court Square chestnut tree. Its aging truck is thick and torn: ragged by storm and darkened by car exhaust. Sandwiched between parking lots and historic buildings for untold seasons, it still stands. And for today, for this hour, for this moment, so too does my mother.

Sheltered as a spring bud in her youth, Mom came of age as America came into war, leaping into the unknown, just like her country. She learned to drive along the few miles that gas rationing would take her. She learned to dance in the arms of boys in pressed uniforms. She learned to work in an office with steno pads and adding machines. A month after the big bombs dropped and silenced the fighting, she took her vows as a doe-eyed bride.

Destiny runs deep. The chestnut never learned to be a tree from its wild ancestors; it grew alone, pinched between brick, cobblestone and concrete. But it stayed true to its calling, sending forth its heavy seeds of life every autumn.

My mother's first five seeds died in her womb before they were born. But she never turned away from her own calling and finally bore living fruit - my brother, sister and me. She patiently taught learning-disabled high school students and by example, she taught us. With her by our side, we braved all our childhood challenges - calming us as we entered our first-grade classroom, coaxing us as we splashed and sputtered in tot swim class at the Y, cheering us at our games, recitals and graduations. Too many to remember, too important to forget. At every twist and turn in life, she was there.

Winter is approaching and the tree's limbs are almost bare. As the shadows deepen, my mother's reality is in flux. She envisions floating images of children and puppies, a horse wearing a red tie. She spits out words as she sleeps; she scratches secret notes that fall off the page. Her glass half-full optimism may be fleeting, but it is not yet empty. We reminisce down well-worn paths of her mind to draw out glimpses of recognition, warmth and wit; we massage cream into frail hands and swelling feet; we kiss her forehead whispering "I love you" and we bite back silent tears as we leave.

Often, she is alone in her thoughts, her dimming eyes staring beyond everyone. Is it her past or her future that she sees? Is her mind replaying sweet, short films, like twirling in a man's embrace or rocking one of her babies in her arms? Or is she searching to find a friendly guardian to illuminate the way? Is she waving hello or a halting good-bye?

The chestnut stretches in the wind and reaches for the sky.

So too does my mother. And some season soon, she will fly.

How our judges and readers responded...

The beautiful image of the Court Square Chestnut tree anchors this piece. Through it we see the way in which your mother influences not only her own history, but also the history of an entire community. ♥ This piece reveals a life beautifully rendered and incredibly full. ♥ You have written a beautiful tribute to your mother. And you have expressed your appreciation and love for her to the end.

BIO:

I am new to Charlottesville. I moved here this fall to help with my mother's care and to be closer to family. I appreciate this opportunity to honor a woman of courage I love and respect: my mother, as she faces life's ultimate challenge.

Challenge into Change

Dysphoria
Roxana Trujillo

What is Gender Dsyphoria?
It is the feeling that everything in this world seems split in two
Things for and by boys and girls
Men and women
Ideas of anatomically predisposed natures
Ways of thinking
Being
Acting
Taking up space
Breathing
Exercising
Swimming
Walking
Throwing
Urinating
Fucking
Sleeping
Talking
Thinking
Drinking
It is always fighting
With others
With yourself
It is knowing you don't always fit in one category at a time
Sometimes fitting both, sometimes neither.
If mother nature didn't do her duty, father nurture will.

Unconsciously, gender dysphoria is knowing you're different
And perhaps thinking something is wrong with you.
Consciously, it is discovering this is all an imaginary game
But oddly enough everyone is following and enforcing the rules
It is knowing that everyone can cris-cross the boundaries if they so
wished

Fearing rejection, you can't
Because the lines around you were drawn before your existence
You were simply born into them
Literally
And when you started to crawl
They steered you away
Stopped you from getting to close to the cusp of the Other
For your own "safety" of course
And as you started walking
They guided you too
Run fast, as fast as you can
But never fast enough
To flee from their plan
Even if they let you be free in your early years
They kept you on a loose leash.
As you matured but did not outgrow your wild
And "different" ways
They gently tugged you back in
After a tug, no change.
Then a firm pull, then a drag.
Finally they lassoed you,
And harshly reeled you in.
"Now that's the last straw!"
That day you learned who governs
'Cause the majority makes the rules
And it's only for what's best
For you
For all
For your protection.
Despite your protestations
You've become and obedient actor of this play
You stay on your side of the stage
Stick to your roles and tricks
The "Other" hides in the shadows
And every once in a while
When they're all looking away

Challenge into Change

You wander yonder
and be free
Ripping of the sheep's skin to reveal the beautiful beast within
Those moments of bliss in a lonely closet you be
Oh what glee!
Can I live like this?
As the fears return
You remember how hard it would be
Reluctantly redressing into to your assigned costume
You dutifully return to flock once again.

Nostalgia for your days as a young child
You reminisce on your times in the school yard
Where it didn't matter boy or girl
It mattered only how good you played, how fast
And then you think, maybe, just maybe if I'm good enough
They'll accept my truths
Your daydream session interrupted by those dreaded lines again
"That's for chics"
"Only guys do that"
Not knowing
who
or what you are
makes you wrestle with yourself on the daily
You surrender to answers unknown
remain silent
Keep moving
Surviving
Till the moment comes
Where the answers set you free
To fully be.

How our judges and readers responded...

How would it feel to live in a world where the only social boundaries that matter reinforce kindness to others and love for all? In this poem, the author calls into question some of society's deepest divisions with at times playful, at times earnest, and always sharp writing. ♥ *So few of us know about gender dysphoria despite it being in the news. Your poem can lead others to understanding.* ♥ *This piece has an intensity that carries the reader. It is affecting, disturbing, and moving.* ♥ *Your heart goes out to the confusion the author feels struggling to conform to norms while feeling like the norms are reflective of who she is.*

BIO:

I'm a gender-queer female bodied human. I graduated from the University of Virginia in May 2014. I studied studio art and philosophy. I grew up in a multi-cultural and conservative family. My identity-finding struggles along with my depression have made living autonomously as an adult very difficult. I still depend on family, who I fear I cannot trust for their continued support if I chose to be honest with them about this struggle. The poem represents this.

Bunny
Erin Tucker

Ten years ago, a newly widowed mother of 2, stood in line at our local methadone clinic waiting for her dose. She had been using heroin dealing with the pain of seeing her husband of 26 years dying. She finally decided that if she was going to take care of her children after the death of their father, she needed to get clean.

Cyndi's plan was simple. She would take the methadone for a year, enabling her to stop the heroin cravings and then taper off. When she told the methadone clinic of this plan, they told her that they wouldn't support her in her taper. They believed that she should stay on it. This former beauty queen, the first black beauty queen in the city of Charlottesville Virginia in the 1970's, decided that she would do it herself. She sat in the recliner for a month, in agony until the pain finally passed.

When it did pass, she got up and she got busy. Not only did she raise her children to be assertive, hard-working, caring individuals but she also dedicated herself to taking care of her mother, who was battling her own cancer. Cyndi took care of her mother until her death, beautifully and gracefully. She is now the primary caretaker of her elderly father, who needs constant care. He calls her "bunny" and adores her. The love she shows for this man is evident. She lights up when she talks about him. She is patient and dedicated to him.

She also works full-time as a certified peer recovery specialist. She is responsible for the national program that engages homeless folks experiencing mental illness and addiction with getting services. She is able to use her warm and welcoming personality to engage folks who normally would not trust anyone.

She inspires the community and is often asked to speak wherever she goes. She is the kindest and most optimistic woman that I've met. She goes above and beyond on a daily basis in a selfless manner. She changes lives. The men and women who formerly experienced home-lessness and who are now housed due to her excellent advocacy still receive her encouragement and support to stay in housing.

Cyndi Richardson has dedicated the last decade to helping people. She has transformed a challenge into change and made the world a better place. Cyndi inspires me to transform my challenges into change as well. I am a better person for having her as a close friend, colleague, and confidante. For all of these reasons, I felt drawn to share her story, consensually of course!

How our judges and readers responded...

What an incredible story. It takes so much strength to overcome drug addiction. Your friend not only overcame her problems, but she became a person with the strength and love to help so many others. ♥ *Your friend is the embodiment of "Challenge into Change."* ♥ *Impressive that the writer chose to focus on someone else. A woman with determination and grit.* ♥ *I'm fortunate to work with Cyndi through a leadership program I run. I didn't know this about her but I appreciate that she let the writer share a bit of her story.* ♥ *"Bunny" is a beautiful tribute to a woman who changed her family and community by facing her own challenges with grace and power. The words weave an inspiring narrative of rising from the ashes to burn bright with a light that shines on and guides others to a hopeful tomorrow.*

BIO:

Erin Tucker works in wellness at On Our Own, Charlottesville. Some of her wellness tools include walking in nature, tarot, transparency, and reading. She has been active in her recovery for many years. She is an organizer of the Twin Oaks Women's Gathering and identifies strongly as a feminist. She has 3 beautiful children, wonderful part-ners, and friends.

Challenge into Change

I Am . . .

Shrika Turner

I am a strong, loving, caring, proud mother
I wonder where I would be without my children.
I hear sweet lullabies when my babies cry.
I see the light at end of the tunnel where we eat funnel cakes
on the beach in the summer
I want my children's futures to be as bright as a summer's day.
I am a strong, loving, caring, proud mother.

I pretend that the darkness is my shadow.
I feel warm inside but cold to touch.
I touch the hearts of so many in life.
I worry about the things that I will not change.
I cry each time my children make me proud.
I am a strong, loving, caring, proud mother.

I understand they will grow old and move on.
I say it won't hurt, but I know I'll be torn.
I dream they grow and reach their goals.
I try to teach the love, respect and discipline- a right way of life.
I hope that I've taught them enough rules of life
that they'll forever live by when times get tough.
I am a strong, loving, caring, proud mother.

How our judges and readers responded...

Beautiful use of repetition—it sounds like a mantra that you can repeat to yourself when you need a little bit of extra strength. ♥ *The line "I pretend that the darkness is my shadow" uses language in a lovely, imaginative way—halfway between metaphor and personification. Really cool!*

BIO:

I am the mother of four beautiful children ages 3 to 10 and student at TJACE. I want to become a registered nurse. I have lived in Charlottesville all my life. I love that the city has grown and that the Downtown Mall is vibrant. I always strive for greatness and love being the role model for my children to grow.

Within ME

Nancy Utz

Within me lies a Dragon.
She has laid sleeping for many a year.
Ones have tried to slay her…
With hurtful words, unsubstantiated accusations, force
Manipulation and even violence
BUT NO MORE!
Within me this Dragon has awakened..
And will tolerate no more abuse of any kind on any level.
Meanness and abuse on any level is Wrong.
Wrong is Wrong
Especially to women and children.
Tolerate NO DARK ARROWS!
Within me lies a Dragon.

How our judges and readers responded…

The metaphor of the dragon makes your strength apparent to the reader. ♥ *The use of pace and the rhythm in these lines shows real poetic skill. Within so many of us resides a dragon.* ♥ *Thank you for expressing the problem of anger so poetically.*

BIO:

I have worked for the Natural Resources Conservation Service as a conservationist for over 34 years. I have lived in Madison County all my life ending up in the same house where I grew up. I live at the foothills of the Blue Ridge Mountains in the middle of a cow pasture with 3 cats and a dog. My daughter is now a young woman on her own. My biggest gift of all.

Untitled
Scott Van Dorn

What I remember from that night, when she hurt so badly that she cut herself, was waking up on the sofa, seeing her and shouting her name so loudly that the knife fell from her hand. That night, I remember feeling completely helpless as some a brute, impersonal force sent her spiraling into a world so far away from mine that afterwards the thousand-yard stare facing me couldn't have been traversed by any number of touchdowns.

"There was so much pain, I didn't know where else to put it except myself," I remember her say, later, the new day just beginning to touch the cold windows with light.

That quote stuck with me, even years later, after we broke up. Once, during a guided meditation on grief, I was instructed to become the embodiment of grief, and then to release everything as I fell into a vast space, without a target (Like morphing into the teardrop of an invisible giant?). This connected instantly: What would it take for her to find a place for her pain that had no target? How do you surpass the tendency for pain to make a target of yourself?

The pain she felt, though, and its aftershocks, was hard and real. Beyond anything I could say to help her, or that I could really comprehend. After all, I had never lost an immediate family member, let alone my father. Imagine: being a 17-year-old girl and losing your father after an unexpected blizzard hits the mountain where he was hiking? The search party scours the area for days while you wait, sleeping alone in your room without pillows or blankets because he has none either? Your birthday passes: they still have no trace. Then, for years you go on telling people that your father isn't dead but "missing" because technically it takes 8 years before a missing person is declared deceased?

And trust me, I looked. The way you look when you think everyone in purple sunglasses must be Bono. Once, I met a backpacker with a similar build and background, and I actually held my breath as I asked him his name.

But while I searched for some miracle happy ending, she had moved on to a greater perspective. Next year will be the 10-year anniversary of his disappearance, and she's no longer looking for her father, nor will she even be in mourning as the decade eclipses. Rather, she told me, she's decided to make it a celebration. A celebration! The hole in her heart – the one I once tried so desperately to cover – she's found the strength to transform it – the something missing became an opening for light to reach her.

As I write this, she's happily living in the dim, cold south of Antarctica, pursuing her career as a female scientist in the interest climate change. No metaphor is lost. Meanwhile, me? I can only remember our time and be glad for what almost seems like no reason at all.

How our judges and readers responded…

A tragedy transformed through story-telling into purpose and reflection. I was in the grip of this story from the very first, vivid line, finding exquisite turns of phrase throughout: "…the new day just beginning to touch the cold windows with light." ♥ The weaving of hard facts with your inner thoughts compelled me along in this narrative, heart-breaking yet graced with the protagonist's strength to change the hole in her heart to "…an opening for light to reach her." ♥ You write so movingly about your friend. You were unable to help her, but she did eventually help herself, and now she helps others…This is the best kind of ending.

BIO:

I live in Virginia, work as a server at The Melting Pot. In 2010 I graduated from Elon University with a degree in Journalism.

Seniors on the Move
Louella J. Walker

We are seniors on the move
Come with us on the Tour Bus
Dressing sharp and looking cool
On the bus there is no fuss.

Well organized trips we take
Get ready and be on time
Come with us and don't be late
Don't come to get the bus at nine.

Laughing, talking with joy is our game.
Wheel chairs and walking canes
The trip will have you saying
I am glad I came.

God has given us a great life
Collecting food for the poor with all our mite.
Serving is our calling you see.
We are very thankful for thee.

With years of wisdom, experiences and knowledge of God
We the seniors are on the accord

We dance, we sing, we let freedom ring
God is in control of everything.

Challenge into Change

How our judges and readers responded...

This is a beautiful, uplifting poem. ♥ *I love how all stanzas adhere to the same structure, but each expresses something new.*

BIO:

I am a widow, was married to the late George R. Walker, for 48 years. This union had three children. I have six grandchildren. I retired from the University of Virginia after 50 years of service. My hobbies are singing, sewing, writing poems, visiting friends and helping people. I attend Mt. Zion 1st African Baptist Church, Charlottesville, VA.

Solid Oak
Erin Newton Wells

Do I call her a grandmother-in-law? I'll call this woman a bonus I received when I married. She anchored the family. On visits home, we always spent a good portion of time with her.

Her first grandchild, my husband, named her Nano, and then everyone called her that. Entering her house was like stepping back to an earlier day where it was safe and warm. We were students then, struggling to make ends meet. But when Nano gave me her strong hug and patient smile, problems fell away.

We sat in the big oak rocking chairs in her living room and talked about old times. She pretty much raised my husband in his younger years while his mother and father worked, and she had many stories to tell of that. Or we sat at the kitchen table, with its oil cloth cover. I studied the ancient things she still used, the heavy stove, gadgets out of the past. The soothing talk went on.

At meals, we sat around the dining table. I ran my fingers over the rows of tiny dark dots that spread everywhere across the oak surface. What were they? My husband told me the story. The dots were made by a star-shaped wheel rolled on the outlines of patterns to transfer the shapes to cloth. Nano had been a seamstress, making clothes for people in the town, stitching her family back together and keeping them whole with this skill.

The grandfather-in-law we never met died in an oilfield accident, leaving a wife and three young children on their own. She was determined to survive, "not be beholden," as she said. An aunt described the many nights she saw her mother working late at this table and the sewing machine beside it. She said the dining room of her childhood smelled like cloth, pattern and transfer paper, and sewing machine oil.

All three children were fed, clothed, their needs attended to. All three were put through college by their mother's efforts. College was the way out. She never had that chance but made sure each of them did.

I admired the bib apron Nano wore, so she made one for me, a small version of her larger one. I treasured every stitch for what it represented. I wore it for years, then kept it when no longer wearable.

When she died, we were given our choice of her things. We selected several pieces from the kitchen. And, of course, we wanted that dining table. It had been re-varnished many times to a dark coffee color. We were hesitant to strip off the layers of history. But when we did, we found the original golden oak beneath, durable and beautiful, ready for many more years. Across it, the darker tracks of the pattern wheel stood out even better. Sand them off? Never. These are a gift, a symbol of why that part of the family continues and thrives. We use the table every day.

How our judges and readers responded...

I love how this story explores the history of what at first seems to be a simple household item. ♥ *Through reading this story, we learn that a kitchen table is not just a place to eat, but can also be a symbol of hard work and dedication.* ♥ *Your continued use of the table proves that your grandmother-in-law's legacy lives on.*

BIO:

Erin Newton Wells has taught studio art many years in a school she established in Charlottesville, Virginia. It has been her privilege to encourage others to recognize their own creative abilities and to achieve the sense of accomplishment they find with this form of expression. She is also a writer, concentrating mainly on poetry, but writes fiction and nonfiction as well. She finds the degree of observation needed and learned both through art and writing extends to so many other areas, especially in listening to and understanding other people.

Challenge into Change

ACKNOWLEDGEMENTS

The Women's Initiative honors the efforts of all of those who generously and bravely shared their stories of healing and transformation with us. Your words have the power to inspire many. Thank you.

Thank you to our panel of judges who held each of these very personal stories with openness and grace. Your expertise, time and care are so deeply appreciated: Karen Boeschenstein, Russell Carlock, Andrea Copeland-Whitsett, and Judith Hannah Weiss.

We are also grateful to our volunteer readers, whose beautiful feedback adds so much to the spirit of this project: Stephanie Bernhard, Alyssa Collins, Anastatia Curley, Maya Hislop, Karen Huang, and Cathryn McCue.

Thank you to the Festival of the Book—particularly Jane Kulow, Sarah Lawson, and intern Allison Elder—for their steadfast support all year.

We also deeply appreciate the Jefferson School African American Heritage Center for co-hosting our award ceremony.

Thank you to our Festival of the Book featured author, Seema Reza, for sharing your wisdom with our staff and with our authors.

Special thanks to the Challenge into Change Committee, without whom this program would not be possible: Tonia Alexander, Katelyn Durkin, Kathleen Ford, Meg Handelsman, and Nancy Summers.

And our work would not be possible without the efforts of The Women's Initiative's program partners, donors, and volunteers, who support us in countless ways.

Challenge into Change

Challenge into Change

MEET OUR JUDGES

KAREN BOESCHENSTEIN

Having evaluated applications for the University of Virginia's Office of Admissions for twenty-three years, Karen Boeschenstein has read thousands of essays. Still, judging the submissions to the Challenge into Change competition was a powerful reminder of the importance of personal stories and an honor she will not soon forget.

RUSSELL CARLOCK

Russell Carlock teaches US history and ESOL at Albemarle High School and serves on the equity and diversity counsel for Albemarle County Public Schools. He also serves on the board of the International School of Charlottesville and coordinated the ESOL and world languages programs for Albemarle County Public Schools, where he helped to develop the Spanish and French language programs in three county elementary schools. He earned his doctorate from the Harvard Graduate School of Education. His research focuses on the ethnographic study of community organizing, parent engagement in education, and the experiences of multilingual students in schools. His teaching and research are motivated by a desire to improve equity in educational opportunity in communities of linguistic, socioeconomic, and ethnic diversity.

ANDREA COPELAND-WHITSETT

Andrea Copeland-Whitsett is the Director of Member Education Services of the Charlottesville Regional Chamber of Commerce, overseeing the Chamber's signature program, Leadership Charlottesville, as well as the Chamber Business Academy, and is the Chamber liaison for the Chamber Business Diversity

Council and Leadership Charlottesville Alumni Association. Andrea is also the founder and president of Positive Channels, a company with a mission to use the power of the media for good. Through Positive Channels, she has interviewed, covered, worked with and met some high-profile figures including President Obama, the Dalai Lama, Star Jones, Sean Penn, civil rights icons Ernie Green, Julian Bond, John Lewis, and more. A native of Charlottesville, Andrea graduated from Charlottesville High School and Piedmont Virginia Community College with an AS in Education. She went on to graduate from Old Dominion University with a BS in Human Services Counseling.

JUDITH HANNAH WEISS

Judith Hannah Weiss worked on staff at Time Inc. and freelanced promoting media for Children's Television Workshop, Disney-ABC, BBC, HBO, PBS and CBS. She earned a BA from Sarah Lawrence College and (briefly) attended Columbia. She worked in Manhattan, lived 24 miles north in an old farmhouse - and then moved to a farmhouse in Virginia. She also creates art for humans, and homes for birds. She won second place in the 2015 Challenge into Change Writing Contest.